Reverence

A priest's life of holiness and humanity

— MAGDALEN SMITH —

Sacristy
Press

Sacristy Press
PO Box 612, Durham, DH1 9HT

www.sacristy.co.uk

First published in 2024 by Sacristy Press, Durham

Scripture quotations, unless otherwise stated, are from the New Revised
Standard Version Bible: Anglicized Edition, copyright © 1989, 1995
National Council of the Churches of Christ in the United States of
America. Used by permission. All rights reserved worldwide.

Every reasonable effort has been made to trace the copyright holders
of material reproduced in this book, but if any have been inadvertently
overlooked the publisher would be glad to hear from them.

Sacristy Limited, registered in England & Wales, number 7565667

British Library Cataloguing-in-Publication Data
A catalogue record for the book is available from the British Library

ISBN 978-1-78959-361-7

Reverence

A priest's life of holiness and humanity

— MAGDALEN SMITH —

Sacristy
Press

Sacristy Press
PO Box 612, Durham, DH1 9HT

www.sacristy.co.uk

First published in 2024 by Sacristy Press, Durham

Sacristy Limited, registered in England & Wales, number 7565667

British Library Cataloguing-in-Publication Data
A catalogue record for the book is available from the British Library

ISBN 978-1-78959-361-7

*This book is dedicated to four people who walked
with me through a time of great pain and darkness.
Some of this book was born during that time.*

Demelza Rouncefield—my second cousin

The Revd Lorraine Reed—friend and former colleague

*The Rt Revd Peter Price—spiritual director and
friend, former Bishop of Bath and Wells*

The Most Revd Dianna Gwilliams—former Dean of Guildford

Contents

Introduction

I have stepped out of my life as priest in a busy urban parish just for a few days. Either by choice or no choice, it is good to stand at the edges and try to discern what is going on in the middle, when we have become too close to a role or persona and it clouds the clarity of who we are. We see, as St Paul says in 1 Corinthians 13, through a glass but darkly.

I am at the marvellous Gladstone's Library, North Wales, having won a scholarship to finish this book. It is an astonishing space which would not be out of place in a Harry Potter sequel. With its two-floor level of carved wood and lots of books, the library draws a global clientele that the nineteenth-century prime minister would never have imagined. His legacy—to create a library accessible to others. Mary, his wife, is quoted on one of the posters hung along the main corridor, "Mr Gladstone often pondered how to bring together readers who had no books and books who had no readers . . . a plan evolved for a country house for the purposes of study and research." Over 80 years old, Gladstone endowed the library with 20,000 books from his home at Hawarden Castle a stone's throw away. But for many years the library did not take his name and was known as the humbler "St Deiniol's Library", after the first Bishop of Bangor in the sixth century.

I have a personal connection to being here which feels especially fitting as I bring to fruition this book—a personal memoir as well as reflection on how it feels to live a current vocation as a cleric. My father was Deputy Warden (in an era when there were such people) here in the 1950s. It was where he met my mother, who came on her days off from Liverpool and her demanding job in social work. Her lifelong fascination with theology and my father's growing reputation as writer and the gravitas he carried (he was 20 years her senior) developed into much canoodling around the roaring fire. More of an old boys' club at that time, my father left, no longer committed to bachelor academia, and the rest, as they say, is history.

There are many in our society who continue to be fascinated by the world of the clergy. Whilst *The Vicar of Dibley* and *Father Brown*, along with errant and vulnerable priests from TV series like *Grantchester* and *Rev* have become national treasures, there have been few memoirs by contemporary clergymen over the years, and even fewer, if any, by clergywomen. A few famous names have biographies to their name— Mervyn Stockwood and Rowan Williams among others—but in 1994 Mary Loudon wrote *Revelations: The Clergy Questioned*. It was a book which interviewed well-known and not so well-known clerics as well as women on the brink of ordination. All of them held different perspectives of who God might be, charting well the wide diversity within a denomination renowned for its grey generosity in encompassing a variety of views. It felt a brave book at the time and one of the few written by a woman. Loudon was able to offer a less cerebral and more existential and interesting record as a result. For women can be naturally good at fusing all the elements of their humanity together. Around the same time in America, Kathleen Norris wrote *The Cloister Walk*, a frank diary of one year of her life, living alongside a Benedictine community. Within its pages, she recorded the liturgical year, its rituals, prayers, and daily activities as she also reflected on her own marriage and vocational purpose. Through her accessible prose and the stories she tells a seemingly impenetrable world becomes immediate and relevant to people of all faiths and none. In both these books, I discovered great richness which eventually led me to want to write my own. I do so too because, like them, I continue to believe that this kaleidoscopic and ever-changing life the clergy live holds a relevance and a beauty which can be used to illuminate what happens in others' lives too.

I have lived this life for all my life. I was a child of the vicarage, met a man who became a priest for 20 years, and before that, I became one of the women in the early days of women's ordained ministry. I was only 26. For much of the world this still feels like an unusual profession; it stimulates fascination with the inevitable question that arrives next at the checkout or on the train, "Why?" The official discernment process aside, I have asked myself that question often and believe it is healthy to keep asking it. Recently my husband decided to have a career change, discovering a new vocation in a brand-new profession. It's brought refreshment to our family—a new world to relate to—rather than simply the Church with a capital "C". And it's brought home, just how introspective and pontifical that capital C institution can often be. The Church and its workings remain anathema, a complete mystery and irrelevance to so many "outside", for the Church uses language like this often as if, like the original St Deiniol's Library, it is some kind of old-fashioned club.

But I want to distinguish between negativity and reality. For despite the catastrophic failings of the Church, the world still needs communities to work out faith and spirituality alongside others. Nick Cave, Australian musician and writer, said recently in a podcast, "I'm not spiritual, I'm religious", a witty reversal of what is the more usual "I'm not religious, I'm spiritual" clarion-cry of our person-centred age. Cave quantifies this by saying, "Religion is spirituality with discipline".* Through that he is expressing that many need to "put their faith somewhere", within the framework of an institution where others have put theirs before. The history and its legacy are rich, of ordinary men and women living immanence and experiencing transcendence in a multitude of ways. Through doctrine and theology many make sense of the questions we cannot answer and of the sense of mystery which lies in the very depths of who we are. The clergy are often leading lights in all of this.

When we experience great pain, it often causes us to reflect differently upon what has been and to ask questions of our lives we have not previously asked. So, I have wondered, in the light of my own children's career choices, in my husband's change of direction, whether I entered this life with a genuine calling as we describe it in our profession, or whether I entered this because of a grief I did not express at the time. My father died when I was only 17 (he was 70). I had led a sheltered existence in Cornwall, a place that I perceived to be furthest away from "the rest of the world". Those two factors meant I dispensed with my passion to act and go to drama school and ventured into a profession which would

---

* Nick Cave in conversation with Krista Tippett on Being podcast *Loss, Yearning and Transcendence*, 22 November 2023.

provoke interest simply because it was an atypical path for young women to walk down at that time.

But it was also far more than this. For my own vocation felt and looked different from the priesthood and ecclesial perspectives of my parents. I dispensed with the Victorian morality of being a good girl and equated the striving for justice in whatever form, with being the primary task of a Christian person and especially a leader. I also held, from an early age, an intuitive fascination with the belief that every human person also has the potential for spirituality, and I saw a myriad of possibilities of expression for that. Faith for me was not a separate part of my being, but was instead like good spices, something which enhanced and brought colour to the rest of my life. I loved the richness of different kinds of people, of experiencing their cultures and liked the idea that a priest, just through presence alone, was called to live alongside others, especially those poor, forgotten and sad through their still beautiful lives. That felt and continues to feel like a massive adventure.

And apart from a sorry 18 months, when a few in power were savage and unfair to myself and family, living this life has been kind to me. The Church has sheltered me, provided me with a home, a steady income, and a happy existence with many opportunities to rest, to study, to travel and to experience different ways of "being church". I would not be here now if it wasn't for a colleague in my diocese encouraging me to apply for a writing scholarship. The Church as institution provided a pension for my mother for over 35 years. I have enjoyed many a fascinating conversation along the way, the collar opening doors for the most part.

Although I have toyed recently with following my brave husband into something entirely different in the last 15 years of a working life—art dealer perhaps (I have a degree in Art History), chef (I love food), or tree surgeon (I like walking in forests and being outside)—I have worked out from the edges here that I need to stay right where I am. For this is also about distinguishing what is the difference between a job and a calling. I arrived here tired, weary of closed and rapidly disintegrating buildings where most weeks one of the old iron pipes cracks and there is yet another water leak. I am weary of people unable to make decisions or working out their personal neurosis and issues, loading onto me the responsibility which should really be theirs. I am tired of being careful of every word I speak, of not forgetting something, of living with the underlying weighty yet unspoken role of being the Parish Saviour. But like King Canute I cannot hold back the tide which is decline. Nationally the Church is shrinking as well as panicking, throwing money and resources at ventures which makes itself feel better, at least temporarily. But I'm wondering if what is needed is to be brave—to bless this decline and to know that God is in it. To know that what we are being asked to find is the stuff of God's kingdom in the tiny emergence of fragile things and events and conversations which contain the secrets of what it means to be human. Jesus did this every single day.

And priests are rare "catch all" people. They are both appreciated and recognized by many as well as being scorned and anathema to others. They are people who can identify the moments where some sense of the divine pervades, people who can extract the mud from the depths as well as illuminate the light from the stars, in any one life. Priests can make connections with the existence of a faith which is often already there. Faith often grows, but often it does not need to be brought in from somewhere else. A priest's calling is to be inquisitive, to ask, "Tell me who you are." For me, the job is not to tell people what to believe, and it is not to impose upon them who God thinks they are. I see my job as helping people to change how they look at the world and each other, to try to retain the love already in their lives and to connect this with a vision of revolutionary love that is at the heart of our faith, as it also is in many others. But I do this, as Christian, through the lens of the story of Jesus Christ and the rich tapestry of the holy ones throughout history who have gone before me as well as those who live still.

There remain essentially three modes of operating pastorally as a cleric—responding to pain, to joy and to wondering (faith and doubt). Through all of this I never tire of doing what the twentieth-century German–American theologian Paul Tillich so exquisitely describes. In fact, he nails it for me:

> Grace strikes us when we are in great pain and restlessness. It strikes us when we walk through the dark valley of a meaningless and empty life. It strikes us when we feel that our separation is deeper than usual, because we have violated another life, a

life which we loved, or from which we were estranged. It strikes us when our disgust from our own being, our indifference, our weakness, our hostility, and our lack of direction and composure have become intolerable to us. It strikes us when, year after year, the longed-for perfection of life does not appear, when the old compulsions reign within us as they have for decades, when despair destroys joy and courage. Sometimes at that moment a wave of light breaks into darkness, and it is as though a voice were saying, "You are accepted. *You are accepted*, accepted by that which is greater than you, and the name of which you do not know. Do not ask for the name now; perhaps you will find it later. Do not try to do anything now; perhaps later you will do much. Do not seek for anything; do not perform anything; do not intend anything. *Simply accept the fact that you are accepted!*" If that happens to us, we experience grace.

After such an experience we may not be better than before, and we may not believe more than before. But everything is transformed. In that moment, grace conquers sin, and reconciliation bridges the gulf of estrangement. And nothing is demanded of this experience, no religious or moral or intellectual presupposition, nothing but acceptance.[*]

Yesterday in the Anglican lectionary the Church remembered George Herbert, faithful priest, writer of hymns and poems and generally good chap. Herbert is known for his book *The Country Parson*, which offers practical advice to rural clergy and was written within the single context of Bemerton, outside Salisbury, where he remained for his entire ministry. Herbert grew a reputation as a holy man and he was an early advocate of understanding ordinary life as being infused with the holy, in his case the implements of the earth—ploughs, yeast and dancing. This simple idea of learning to read the contexts and cultures of where we land as clergy, of glimpsing grace and beauty in those we serve, of preaching hope in acceptance as Tillich does, remains at the heart of what a priest does. It

---

[*]   Paul Tillich, *The Shaking of the Foundations* (London: Penguin, 1963), p. 163f.

is about being real with others who come but who cannot articulate or unlock the hollowness they feel inside. It is about opening our hearts to people in their unvarnished states, of vulnerably sharing our own stories and of being kind.

The parish where I currently minister is a bohemian one. Birmingham is an oft-misunderstood city, but I have grown to love its dirty pavements, international cuisine and its creative vibrancy. My churches hold a transience, as does the city, where people arrive and state, they will make this their home. We are good at welcome; the congregation here have developed a well-honed attitude of acceptance and non-judgment, as they, unfazed by the damage and colourful idiosyncrasies of tattoos and Tibetan pants, provide tea and human warmth. Many have worked for years in a city where they have experienced and managed much poverty and brokenness within those in their care, and so they understand. But many who walk through the doors do not stay too, or simply reside for a time and take what they need. For my people this matters not; they are too full of love and possibility at the potential of those who come.

I have learnt to understand this bubbling brook of goodness which flows underneath the sharp words or the flurry of frustration of our regular congregation. For I know they know what it means to live a life which offers grace and a chance for others. There is a very great amount of love and openness, especially towards those who fall through the sieve of society's care systems and the church is often the only place which is prepared to scoop them up.

Our roles and vocations ebb and flow as we are simultaneously beaten down with compassion fatigue, perhaps reprimanded by those in authority, as well as encouraged by occasional glittering successes. What tires me at times is that things can move so slowly in the Church of England for we are for ever bound by archaic rules and are now drowning in bureaucracy surrounding ancient buildings and keeping people safe. The job these days at the coalface can feel weighty and often lonely, impossibly complex and often misunderstood, a glorified, religious social worker that simply rocks up on Sundays. And within the ranks we argue about everything that feels important to those on the inside of Church when the rest of the world cannot for the life of it understand why we are still discussing issues everyone else takes as read.

Yet the truth remains that there are few things I would rather do. The Church of which I am a part continues to feel a bit like a party I can't quite leave. Recently I have tried to be better at affirming those tiny things I or we do as a community that make a difference even if this is never recognized or recorded. The story of Joe speaks into this. A mother from down south contacted me via the parish website about her son. Would there be any volunteering opportunities for him, a young man in his thirties who was lonely? There are always things people can do and sometimes that takes a little effort to organize the right people to connect with alongside the right tasks. And I have an issue with anyone described as lonely and church communities can be good at helping with this, even a little. I encourage people to come and be part of "us", regardless of belief or experience. And I did this with Joe too as we met in our quiet chapel where he met our church warden and other members of staff. Volunteering was set up and, wracking my brains in my cup-half-full way, I invited him on the parish walk a few of us would do that coming Saturday afternoon. "It will be mostly women in their fifties and above, you know, but come anyway; you are welcome." Joe showed up; we walked along the canal into the refurbished Gas Street, had a cuppa and walked back. Everyone on the walk made some kind of effort to talk to him. He seemed to enjoy it and I was pleased when our site manager told me he had arranged to meet him for some gardening. But Joe never arrived and a week or so later I emailed his mother just wondering . . . ? I know how hard it can be to re-cross the threshold once you have not done something promised. She emailed back to tell me that Joe had died suddenly last weekend. Shocked and saddened, as were others I told, we did not know anything of the circumstances. I had sensed when we met that he had been troubled in some way. But his mother continued in further exchange, "Joe found much solace in his encounters with you all and appreciated the kindness. He was enjoying getting to know you." He had been reading Ecclesiastes as a book to bring to our termly book club. Knowing the philosophy of this particular biblical book made my heart break a little.

This is just one of many tiny pearls, luminescent but grown with grit, of how a community can make a difference to a human life, even in a very short time. Joe's story with us has no grand outcome; it cannot become a mission statistic but for me it shows me something of how God works and of why I still inhabit this role of priest. It is about the giving of chances, providing opportunities, listening and including. These things are continuous verbs in church life, and as leaders we shape and influence how those who are brave enough to sit in the pews look at their lives. For this life continues to be so beautiful and compared to many, such a privilege. For it is a fortunate thing to feel like you are making some kind of difference, to be satisfied in your profession, for that to be delightfully unpredictable and for you to enjoy job security more than most. This book then is the story not only of my life, the origins of why I decided to take the step I did, but also of how it feels to live it right now. It is also the story of many of the incredible people I have met and continue to meet along the way and of how they show me something of the nature of who God might be too.

1

An unusual path

I remember the moment I decided to become a priest. It felt exhilarating, like the one and only time I have danced in the rain as that warm deluge soaked both me and an equally mad housemate one summer night. In the dusty hot days of confused youth, the thundery clouds of female emancipation had finally arrived in the Church. But that story had been brewing for years and, like an impending downpour, the pressure finally broke. I had refound my faith just at the moment when women were "let in" to become fully fledged priests. I was young, pretty and slightly wild, my name suggesting the kind of woman some men might feel ambiguous towards. I was enthusiastic, edgy, perceived perhaps to be a mover and shaker. The call had built, like those storm clouds, grown out and away from a rebellion of childhood faith which was equated with being good. Now, belief had been owned and honed by a new vision which felt lifegiving, distinctive, discovered through the wisdom found in words from the past, from prophets of the present and from listening to stories of injustice and what the Bible says about that. Was it God who put the dream in my heart, those books in my hand, the people in my pathway? Or was it a hereditary instinct to be different, safe in the ark yet also, like Noah or Jonah, some kind of inadvertent trailblazer?

How do we choose a life? Some people pursue the dream they have always had, clinging to it like a prized possession whilst others fall into a life accidently. For years I wanted to be an actor, finding a strange solace, as well as the opportunity to inhabit the limelight by acting in school plays. Acting, I discovered, was a way to build self-esteem whilst also being someone else. Actors are praised for their versatility if they are truly great, but it takes a skilled interviewer to perceive the real personality beyond what is seen on the screen or stage. But just before my sixteenth birthday I realized I no longer had the courage to cope with the acting life. I sensed its insecurity as much as I was attracted to its craft. I knew that I was someone more conservative than I could then admit, knew that I craved the stability of a different existence, mourning the priest-father I lost at 17, himself the provider of a clergy life and its strange securities.

Yet after three years of an arts degree, I had worked through some of the religious rebellion of my late teenage years. I dispensed with the idea of assessing, selling and curating objects from an art history degree and decided that my true calling was to be a priest. Pursuing this dream, ridiculous to many and intriguing to others, put me right back in the spotlight I had lost whilst treading the boards. It was a heady mix of building the ego with a genuine sense of wanting to live some kind of meaningful life.

Some say there is a connection between the three professions of acting, the law and being clergy and all have been present as professions in my own family. All three require an upfront, public presence of some description, all include costumes of the trade to help "inhabit" roles. Or, if cynical, those uniforms of office help to project authority as well as trust and, at times, enable a certain hiding behind the role. For some it becomes easy, in dog-collared shirt or cassock to put on that strange clergy persona that masks the vulnerability of the person beneath. And priests, like lawyers and actors, have to work hard to balance this sense of genuineness—being the Revd—whilst allowing who we really are to not just shine through but to breathe. We fight often to shed the skewed and inherited prejudices which have formed over years, or which can build so quickly. "Being authentic" feels at times an unnecessary burden and something which takes a lifetime to live well.

The word vocation comes from the Latin verb *vocare* which means "to call" and assumes a sense that something "out there" (call it God, divine power, or our deep-seated conscience) pulls or pushes us to do something specific, for good. This feeling usually grows and often becomes so strong we cannot seem to put it down. We feel compelled or duty-bound to pursue it, often at all costs and against the odds. A "vocation" certainly in the Church can also take on a gargantuan sense of importance. I know because I have worked in the field of ecclesiastical vocations for some years. Assessing an ordained vocation in the Church has become complicated and can take a very long time. It feels to many that only the most worked through and stable individuals can make it in this profession. These days you have to demonstrate every positive adjective under the sun. In my days assessing candidates, I have wept when well-meaning and thoroughly wonderful human beings who talk of sacrifice, service and love are told they do not have a calling to the ordained life. All of this can sometimes feel over scrupulous, and ridiculously cautious.

And we need to be careful. For those living the clergy life can become self-important, for when we carry "a vocation" around like a prized piece of jewellery, it is tempting to set ourselves apart from others or to allow them to put us on a pedestal. It is sometimes forgotten in the clergy world that many people work long, long hours every day, in jobs where being continuously polite to others and absorbing abuse is par for the course. Many also feel called to do something but will never have the opportunity to explore. "Having a vocation" can be a luxury.

But vocation at its best is looking out at the view from a different window. It enables us to live within our lives but to see and respond to that life through a particular lens. It is about glimpsing beauty and soothing pain often in and for people we may never really get to know. It is like the faithful care of nurses who offer physical and emotional compassion to those who might only stay in hospital for a few hours. Finding and living a true vocation whatever that might be is how Ben Okri describes the craft of writing:

> But finding the subject and theme which is in perfect harmony with your deepest nature, your forgotten selves, your hidden dreams, and the full non resonated essence of your life—now that cannot be reached through searching, nor can it be stumbled upon through ambition. That sort of serendipity comes upon you on a lucky day. It may emerge out of misfortune or defeat. You may happen upon it without realizing that this is the work through which your whole life will sing. We should always be ready. We should always be humble. Creativity should always be a form of prayer.*

---

* Ben Okri, *A Way of Being Free* (London: Phoenix House, 1997), p. 15.

Anything important in our life never completely goes away, whether it is born of love or of pain. The stuff of meaning lives within us even if it reshapes, recalibrates, and resurrects. Vocation changes too—it ebbs and flows and sometimes changes direction.

My sense of call began to develop when I was an art student during three glorious autumn months in Venice. Living in that watery paradise meant discovering tiny churches, open and flooded with a sense of sacred hush and surreptitious masterpieces. Vocation, like art, has moments of clear discernment as well as confusion where we struggle at times, to see its shadowed outline. One summer vacation, desperate to travel the world, I journeyed for one month to Burkina Faso, at that time an unusual part of Africa, with a conservative Christian group whose sole aim was to pray for the conversion of that country from Islam to Christianity. The trip proved physically tough as we bumped around on roads untarmacked and indistinct, visiting communities where church was of paramount importance whilst hygiene was not. We camped in the bush, and I contracted dysentery becoming the most ill I have ever been. A theology of spiritual cleansing was suggested—the group had already identified me as the rebel among them and one who needed a bit more Holy Spirit. It was the rainy season and much of that time was spent digging out our truck as it came to a grounded halt in mud. That alone should have been a sign for us of divine resistance to the cause. But through all that a refining happened within who I wanted to be as a person of faith—building an approach of inclusivity of others and dispensing with what I instinctively felt were damaging and unhelpful beliefs.

After university I enjoyed three years exploring and confirming my vocation to be a priest. The first of these years had a deep impact. After graduation I arranged to undertake an intern year in a parish of many cultures and nationalities in Shepherd's Bush, West London, working alongside an old parish priest whom my family had known as a child. Living in a small bedsit in a shared house the parish owned, I supplemented my income by babysitting and a part time job in the nearby supermarket. Very quickly I immersed myself in the life of this vibrant area of the capital. Fr John was an irascible but visionary leader who had links with Namibia and the anti-apartheid movement. In the early 1990s he worked hard at promoting and encouraging the leadership of minority-ethnic members of his congregation. Many of his flock embraced me as one of their own and I enjoyed their expansive hospitality. I ate out most nights in what felt like the parish restaurant—relishing the home cooking of Caribbean, Nigerian, Ghanaian, Sri Lankan and other Londoners.

It was here I learnt to see the beauty and preciousness of people who powerfully made up the rainbow people of what Christians understand as the Kingdom of God. Flo, housebound with her budgie and cluttered flat, and Elsie, her friend whom she both adored and despised simultaneously; Cynthia, the current church warden who educated me in the delights of salt fish and ackee, fried chicken, rice, peas and plantain; and Rex and Celia, teachers who gave me a home on their top floor when I returned to London for a few weeks after the year had ended and who included me in their own family for at least a year. The parish also had a project—the Upper Room—which provided hot food and second-hand clothes to the homeless and which was firmly established in the locality. It was here I also helped and through it understood how social action is a magnet for getting involved in a faith-filled life whatever your doubt or denomination. Through serving here I made the important connection between what happens on the Sunday sharing of bread and wine with a physical feeding and loving of those who are especially broken.

The church itself was Victorian with a brick interior. Liberal Catholic by tradition, Fr John marked the church seasons and significant festivals well. Helping to organize these felt rich and significant—the feeling of wanting to provide such opportunities myself for other Christian people grew in importance. The sanctuary in the church had an enormous metal corona in the form of a crown of thorns which hung over the altar itself. I preached a little, but every week would act as server, and it was being involved in this ritual that I believe my own sense of vocation changed. Each week I watched the numerous nationalities who formed part of St Saviour's congregation troop up to the altar to kneel together to receive Jesus' body and blood. As the weeks went by, I was aware of something deep within me which found this simple act transformational. Here, it seemed, kneeling beneath the crown of thorns, was the place where each person was given dignity and equality through the sacrament. I found myself yearning to be the person who put bread into their hands.

Fr John and I clashed considerably. In the days before General Synod had passed the vote for women's ordination to the priesthood, I regularly sat in meetings where I was the only woman, amongst groups of male clerics, clad completely in black. There were no female role models in those days, and one day John remarked that he did not consider me tough enough for this kind of profession. But none of that deterred me for I had enjoyed and experienced something profound in that place for a year. The call to the ordained life—however improbable—felt now to be something I could not shift although I knew too that I was still not ready to test it out. This grounded and ordinary parish experience had given me a taste of many things—liturgical life, pastoral care and listening to the stories of pain from the Windrush generation and their children. I learnt how it felt to be in a minority as I became a guest at gatherings where I was the sole white person. More than anything I drank up the exquisite beauty within diversity and learnt that the only thing that really matters as a priest is that you love your people.

As part of this I had read Kenneth Leech's *Struggle in Babylon*, the work of an Anglican giant which highlighted the structural racism in the cities and churches of Britain. I had even met up with Ken a few times. He was working in East London and had known my own father who had been a priest and author. Alongside this was a growing interest in the struggles in South Africa as Nelson Mandela had been finally released from prison while I had been at university a few years previously. I flew to Durban to spend a year at a conference centre in KwaZulu on the east coast of South Africa.

2

Fairgrounds and carnivals

I have returned to a city where 20 years ago was also the place I called home. To return has taken me by surprise, like the taste of a long-forgotten recipe from childhood. "Never go back" has been a personal motto for a clergy family who have often moved onwards, living with the open attempt to love a whole load of newness. Some clergy stay in the same place for all their lives, while others practise a peripatetic, nomad-like existence, creating home wherever the job takes them. Mostly friends are found, but occasionally the situation proves disastrous. I have Roma blood in me somewhere down the line; my great grandfather married a traveller, and my mother was a perpetual "mover", retaining the capacity to start again in a completely different place knowing no one. Clergy often remain those on the edge of the inside, strange establishment figures who at the same time can be vilified and misunderstood.

St Patrick was abducted and held captive in Ireland for six years. It was a land of hardship and suffering for him yet, after escaping, this fiery saint chose to return to serve its people and love its land years later. On holiday in Cambodia, I discovered what felt like another strange return in a man who chose to spend his later years in the place where he had been tortured—S21, the infamous prison in Phnom Penh—where victims of the Khmer Rouge were detained before being taken to the Killing Fields. Redemption and forgiveness were smelt in the scented petals of the frangipani tree he sat beneath every day as he chatted and educated the tourists in better times.

Travelling folk return too, year upon year, in a perpetual cycle of roving, even though it is hoped their experience in doing so is not so traumatic as the above stories related. Ironically, an established way of life means transience and a yearning to not stand still. I am fascinated by fairgrounds and generally tend not to be a fan. But a trip to Margate Vintage Fair—Dreamland—made me reflect on this as an analogy not only of clergy life but of many people's experiences of church and of vocation too.

Most people have visited fairgrounds at some point during their lives. It is entertainment for the kids, the thrill of adrenalin-filled rides as well as more sedate pursuits. Some return to church like this too, as faith is reignited either dramatically or more gently through prayer or song or sacrament. Church, like the fairground, is sometimes a nostalgic experience as we remember visiting for the first time as children. Dreamland is set up as a "vintage" fair, a successful attempt to provide some kind of regeneration in a jaded town, the victim of county lines and the desolation of poverty. Perhaps with its Turner Art Gallery and this, it can prove a living resource once again.

The Church of England is tired as well as desperate to recruit, to gather and to remain relevant. Sometimes full of its own self-importance, many still love it and recognize its leaders who, for the most part, seem to inspire a sense of security and goodness in others. Parishes which have few resources have no choice than to mend what is broken as opposed to create something new. It tends to trendify its image, believing it can draw the crowds, that if the ringmaster (or mistress) is glittering enough it can sow the seeds of belief through various kinds of spiritual entertainment.

Fairgrounds are earthy places, often rough round the edges, attracting an assortment of humanity. Clergy cope with this too, people from every section of society and all the stuff which is often broken and unresolved. They listen and navigate the highs and lows in a life, the celebrations, and the desolations too. Ministry can be an emotional roller-coaster as we feel our way, full of empathy to where someone is at any given moment. Our hearts can feel on occasions a sense of confusion as internally we are spun by the turmoil and issues of others just like a ride on the proverbial fairground waltzer.

For many years I worked in the arena of vocation, helping people to discern what they believed God was asking of them at a particular time in their lives. Living a life which feels fruitful and well lived is what all vocation is about, whatever it is we do. Discerning any vocation, any new stage of life when we are at a crossroads is like arriving at a fairground.

There can feel to be so many options, but we quickly decide at least where we do not wish to go. There might be too that sense of experiment—we might try a bit of this or that and usually there is the navigation of what others want and need to do as well, those whose lives are closely intertwined with our own. There is too, like that fast, terrifying ride of Oblivion, a sense of exposing our whole selves.

The step to think about what that might be at any stage in life can be both exhilarating as well as one where many feel a sense of trepidation. Discernment certainly for an ordained calling requires focus and nerve. It means looking at the whole of a life, identifying the strengths and celebrating them, looking for the buzz word of the now—"transferable skills". I loved getting to know a whole heap of interesting people who wanted to live out this strange new calling, who had lived other lives of interest and achievement.

But that journey also required digging up the muck which often proves to be inevitably painful. We must prove, as clergy, that somehow we are stable enough to absorb the instabilities and angst of others all the time. To do this the Church has ways to thoroughly investigate all the shame of a past life, be it a messy divorce or addiction to drugs and often issues which have already been dealt with; it can feel unnecessarily brutal to ask someone to relive the experience again. The vocational journey needs good companionship, and when I was this person for the Church (Director of Ordinands), I attempted to ask the tough questions gently. It reminded me of stepping onto the Big Wheel, something I have failed to persuade any of my family to accompany me on as no one particularly likes heights. But the feeling of "coming full circle" in a life, of undertaking bravely a process which looks at the whole of who we are can be important. And the view from the top can draw fresh inspiration and might provide a new way forward. Even if someone chose not to pursue an ordained vocation, they would comment that they had enjoyed the journey and glimpsed new horizons, often seeing new perspectives on themselves.

Now I have returned to the coalface of parish ministry, my calling feels deeper as well as more expansive. It has returned to simplicity. It finds a presence or an absence of the sacred in most situations in some shape or form. Older now and hopefully wiser, I know where I want to put my energies into in my own calling and where I do not. I want church, like any good fairground, to offer itself unashamedly for what it is. A place where people can come to find wherever their gap is, a bit of sunny companionship in an otherwise lonely life, a sense of ritual and peace, a moral compass, nostalgia, to learn how to pray or a sense of community. My job is to make the connection between life and faith, to draw out where a sense of divine life already is.

When I lived in Birmingham before, I was an intern in a poor inner-city neighbourhood. The priest I was working alongside struggled with long-term fatigue. I was tasked with setting up a community carnival to inject some positivity and affirmation into that place. That event took some organizing and a lot of anxious sweat, but one breezy summer's day a queue of floats with different community groups, steel bands and school kids drove around the area's streets. On the vast green space of no borders in that 1960s urban space was a smorgasbord of stalls offering a variety of food stuffs from around the world, music and activities. It was a day of cheap feel-good treats which drew a crowd. Neither did it matter that I was a young white woman from Cornwall with little experience of diverse cultures and their richness. I sat back with members of our tiny congregation, laughing at the achievement which had brought so much joy, regenerating a small sense of contentment in an otherwise dejected place.

I learnt that the heartbeat of God is strangely connected to everything and that these very ordinary and homemade events are an exquisite demonstration of this. It is tangible to feel, divine life woven into the very fabric of life. Christopher Jamison says of his own calling as a monk that the reason he entered that life is not now the same as the reason he chose to stay.* Somewhere along the way I chose to stay in the Church of England, whatever its dark failings. Not being paid to work that year, I survived on benefits and the generosity of the parish. I lived amongst, offered help, got stuck in, and that is really all that is still needed.

---

*   Christopher Jamison, *Finding Sanctuary: Monastic Steps for Everyday Life* (London: Weidenfeld & Nicholson (Phoenix), 2006), p. 5.

3

Beginnings

The Georgian house where we lived was damp and draughty. It was a beast of a place, its autumn spiders so enormous you could hear their hairy sprints across the floor. Once rats were discovered under the dining room floor, their decomposing, oniony scent unmistakable. My mother had a zero-tolerance on rodents except for my pet hamster, who had been allocated its own room, the former conservatory, where she ran around, blithe and free until she met a drowned doom after a scrambled climb into a watering can.

My mother disliked the house. Being a woman who lived the "cleanliness is next to godliness" ethic, she spent much of her time doing just this, with some local help from Brenda up the road whose daughter was one of my friends. No sooner had she finished the rooms on the third floor, she concluded the bottom ones were dirty again, compelling her to begin all over again, consumed in a perpetual Promethean domestic punishment. Such grandiose residences were not uncommon 40 years ago, but as church finances have dwindled, many of these vicarages have been sold, replaced by more practical but dull four-bedroomed brick abodes. Our house had eight bedrooms and, as an only child, I moved rooms every time I got bored. I accidentally set fire to one room after some candle experiments went wrong, remember suffering with sunstroke in another, and in one, next to the archaic lavatory, I was violently sick after drinking from a stream polluted with sewage whilst out for a walk with friends. The guest room, with its African blanket throws my father had picked up on a lecture tour, was reserved for midnight feasts with a friend from school when she came to stay. To me the house was a mansion of magnificent adventure, but clergy need to think about the future and to housing themselves when they retire. My father, an older dad, was only a few years off retirement, and early in my secondary education we moved to what felt like a tiny home, semi-detached with rowdy neighbours on an ugly estate two miles away from my school. It proved a hard bump away from the privilege as we acclimatized to this new and unexceptional shelter.

Clergy are professional nomads, used to making home wherever the job takes them. We become experts at establishing roots quickly, settling like travellers on land and premises that others often believe they have the right to occupy too. A strange combination of "incomer" as well as establishment figure, some of us stay for lengthy periods in any one place while these days as the job proves relentless and conflictual, we go sooner rather than later, often leaving those in our care confused and frustrated.

My own first clergy home was in marked contrast to the house I spent eight years in as a child—a small flat in a council block on Floor Eight of a high rise just outside Liverpool. Having my own space at last, after years as a student and spiritual wanderer, felt delightfully precious—my own unassuming palace in the sky. The four tower blocks were cared for conscientiously by four caretakers who would (all) be round like a shot if I had any kind of problem. When this happened, they chatted away in that philosophical and distinctive Scouse banter, where life seems hopefully rosy even amidst the greatest of despairs like my flooded washing machine. They enjoyed the fact that a member of the clergy was living in one of their residences, feeling perhaps an inadvertent blessing because of it, and their own presence became one of continual reassurance for me. The flat was accessed by a lift which smelt of both urine and disinfectant and my car got broken into twice while I lived there. It felt an isolated existence in that block with Joanie, a single and cheerful mum who lived next door. But my only disturbances were the occasional rows she had with her boyfriend and the enthusiastic sexual exploits of the couple who lived above.

There are not many professions that still provide housing as part of "the package". The military and some jobs in farming or tied cottages on large estates are some of the others. But with "the vicarage" there is the expectation that the house is part private home and part public space. A clever design means this boundary can be sustained for the most part. I have just got used to this over the years, enjoying welcoming others into the space. But the invasion of others who sometimes assume they have the right can be especially tough for clergy kids who cannot wander around in skimpy clothing just when they please and must be careful with the language they use, continuously guarded. Yet my own children say that the positives still outweigh the negatives. They are aware of the privilege of living in large properties, have enjoyed (mostly) the interaction with all and sundry, recognizing that this has taught them a courtesy and respect for a wide variety of humanity.

Anita Roddick, of Body Shop fame, suggests that home evolves along with our own lives, expanding or contracting the "world" we reside in. She says, "It shifts from something physical to something spiritual . . . In the best of all worlds, home is the nurturing place where mind harmonizes with body and soul."* My last vicarage but one was a busy place, strangers and friends coming and going most days, not to mention the teenagers who used its enormous kitchen to grab a quick bite of breakfast and congregate after school, all friends of my sociable daughter and son. Here grew accidentally the idea that this home provided some kind of haven, a relished space where people could explore their own "soul space" over a cup of tea. The ideal of anyone arriving and discovering another's human warmth on the other side of the door when they need it. That happens often in the popular series *Call the Midwife*, where there is an unspoken and intuitive understanding that whatever it is a person presents as conundrum or desperate plea will be engaged with kindly by the nuns or midwives in its convent, Nonnatus House. And mostly I love it all, except when I am tired, and then I hide in the shadows of the back rooms, ashamedly pretending I am not in simply because the constant demands to be available feel too great.

But welcoming others is an instinctive response in my life. Being interrupted *is* the work of the clergy. Providing a sanctuary where people who need to can be fed with food, friendship or both is inherited from my childhood. My mother, possessing a natural vocation for hospitality, worked hard at organizing large gatherings for my father's colleagues and students. But she also brought back homeless men she found sleeping on

---

*   Anita Roddick, *The Big Issue Book of Home* (London: Hodder & Stoughton, 2000), p. 6.

the church porch, mentally challenged and probably dangerous, seriously pungent and very, very hungry. Seeing a very hungry and very lonely person eat is a spiritual experience, especially when you are six. Never had the roast beef disappeared from our middle-class table so rapidly, and it was weeks until the bathroom recovered its freshness. The closest I have got to that is offering our garage to a man who had nowhere to go on a freezing winter's night, and these days we are advised of course not to jeopardize our personal safety or to blur the boundaries. He weed in the sleeping bag and was gone before I could offer him breakfast. But those memories from my own beginnings cemented a fervent desire to always offer hospitality, albeit in shifting forms and to never take the roof over my head as a given.

Castle, cottage, caravan, or barge, all of us need to have somewhere to call "home", a place of definitive shelter. It is a basic human right. Anxiety over suddenly not having a home or of being unsafe in this sense is a terrible experience. At the height of the Covid pandemic I entered a period where that sense of deep vulnerability arrived at my door too, as my job and the home where we lived became suddenly insecure. I went through an entire year of sustained trauma, wondering what the outcome might be. But as a member of the clergy, that is not a bad experience to live through. Psalm 91 with its verses of promised sanctuary and God's protection were repeated fervently and continually, and it remains a passage in the Bible I often offer to others too. I have subsequently heard the stories too, of other clergy who have had the right to live in their homes removed at short notice. Thanks to the kindness of the local church community, we were given permission to remain in our home whilst my son completed important exams. The cleric responsible for this act of generosity had themselves told me that they had, at one time, been forced to spend a week living from their car with two small children due to their own personal crisis.

To grow up, home also has to be somewhere we have to leave, or at least sit light to. Home is a state of mind, says Roddick. And that's the thing. Now I have honed an attitude of hospitality that I carry around with me, it is a part of me as well as a physical dwelling, a welcome that is offered at the bus stop or in the local shop as well as when my front door physically opens. For many the house they grew up in will be the house they are carried out of. But not so for us, wherever we lay our hat becomes our home and one day it will be nice when this is owned and can be shaped, controlled and where the metaphorical rug cannot be pulled from under our black polished feet.

4

Eden

Inevitably an immense garden wrapped itself around the twenty-three-roomed house of my childhood, and I spent a significant proportion of my time out of doors in this rambling yet safe space. Our vicarage lay at the bottom of a steep street and to the kids who lived there, the garden provided an enticing paradise. Like Eden, it seemed a primeval place of discovery, a space for imaginations to exercise their potential that seems only possible in a young life. I, of course, had free rein at any time, like the mistress of some marvellous stately home, able to explore its delights long after the visitors had returned home. Climbing trees was a particular delight and seated high up in the branches of an expansive chestnut, the sunlight dappled on my skin, became the beginning of a sense of the contemplative.

My mother, a ferocious vegetable grower, supplied our small family with fresh produce every day. The raspberry and strawberry beds were prolific. Friends and I stuffed surreptitious mouthfuls on the dusty summer soil of the fruit garden, red juices dripping down our chins, changing us into vampire children. The garden contained enough fruit trees for it to be designated an orchard, and one year a group of hippies came and gathered up all they could, returning a week later with some dubious looking wine. It made my grandfather ill and got me into trouble, as I smuggled some into school, a group of us getting drunk in a cupboard. During the winter of 1976 we sledged on tin trays, down the steep lawn, with neighbours, then limped in rosy-cheeked, for hot chocolate—a rare luxury. Then, one day, the garden became eerily quiet. Adders had been discovered by a local boy in the wilder and more overgrown bottom section. All was revealed as a dead snake was paraded in a show-and-tell at a whole school assembly. But that temporary embarrassment to my family did not last long—the garden drew its explorers back—too tempting in its hidden promises and endless potential. Soon I was playing hide-and-seek again and rampaging through the long bamboo grove with my mates, spying on the old folks who lived in the home past its jungle leaves.

Most of these larger vicarage gardens are long gone, deemed unnecessary and unmanageable, belonging to an era when clergy wives (always wives then) would work supporting their clergy husbands rather than having a job outside of the home. This was my mother, who thankfully enjoyed gardening, and tended ours in some kind of semi-monastic bliss. These days, with clergy and partners working often in separate careers, they are only just managed, and have grown tired, a bit like the Church itself. One garden where we lived was one such space. Unpruned fruit trees produced copious amounts of apples and pears which remained inedible, a paradise for wasps. In an urban setting it was still a haven, surrounded by the thick hedges of other clerical housing and the extensive, parklike land of a cathedral. We had a family of deer who passed through, timid yet intrepid. In my garden of now skinny foxes regularly forage for scraps, sometimes curling up beneath the hedge, their bronze coats absorbing the free warmth of the sun in an otherwise vilified life. I shouldn't, but I feed them—they are great organic dustbins and will eat anything. I love their rough, furry presence and that the garden provides a natural sanctuary for them. They become symbols of those deserving welcome in church too, those who present to the suited and respectable, a rough and ready challenge.

Gardens in the Bible are described as places of beauty, shelter, innocence and sustenance. They contain a sense of natural abundance in terms of food stuffs—figs, vines, herbs and often a well. The biblical garden of Eden began as a space of delectable lushness and degenerated into a place of pain and shame. In popular culture the concept of Eden is used to describe a place of sanctuary, origin, beauty and productivity. And a natural haven. Certainly, that was true for my mother who found the expected respectability of being a clergy wife oppressive. She found large amounts of people exhausting and found solace over the years in the silence of the garden. Plants, she used to say, are generally rewarding. You tend them, feed them, and they grow. On the whole, they are non-conflictual. You can talk to them and look after them, but they don't take our energy in the way that people do. More than anything perhaps, the garden was a place where she felt able to be herself, and I remember her coming in, muddy jeans and hair unkempt clutching a bunch of prize onions.

But the garden proved to be important to my mother for another reason. Gardens hold atmospheres, they are places which encourage us to "be" as well as "do" and spaces where people find solace in one way or another. Way down the bottom part (where the adders had been found) was an unused hut. My mother cleared this, painted its interior white and made it into what she described as a *poustinia*—in Russian spirituality—a small and sparsely furnished cabin or room where someone goes to pray or fast or to be alone. She was becoming increasingly interested in the Russian Orthodox tradition, moving away from the Church of England where my father worked. The spirituality of the so-named Desert Fathers and Mothers, who removed themselves from the pressures, temptations and trivialities of the world, appealed, as did the depth she could not seem to find in the established Church. There is not so much difference between a *poustinia* like this and any space—man shed or summerhouse—which others use as a retreat from daily life. For her it was also a place to hide.

I have always loved gardens, even though I know little about gardening. Wandering through the different "rooms" of a garden can feel a religious experience. Wild or tamed, gardens have the capacity to draw us into an immersive sensory experience, whether it is by the heady, butter scent of a thousand roses or the fresh dank delight of shrubbery dripping with summer rain. My own love of being outside, breathing the freedom of the air, stems from being a child lucky enough to live in and amongst a large garden like this. Now I identify with so many who say they find God outside too—in the beauty and the challenge of the natural world. John Muir, the "Father of the National Parks", said that he would rather be in the mountains thinking about God than in church thinking about the mountains. On a summer morning when the air is sweet and atmosphere hazy, many would rather find God outside, as there is blessed relief from words and screens and people, and the vistas are long and distant. I don't blame them, for there is a large part of me that knows just what they mean.

Adam and Eve were banished from the biblical Eden because they dared to play God. The fruit from the Tree of Knowledge was just too tempting and they boldly challenged the authority, the ultimate all-knowingness of the divine. Masaccio's *Expulsion from the Garden of Eden*, for me, is one of the most powerful of all representations of this moment as Adam and Eve's desperation and utter dismay is tangibly felt. Adam covers his face and Eve looks as though the world has ended for her. It is a personification of shame. The garden too was where I first discovered this insidious and most powerful of human experiences as I stripped naked for a local boy as he explored (in a different shed) my body and I his. But we were only nine. Other gardens mentioned in the Bible also hint at some of the power of emerging sexuality. In the Song of Solomon, the garden is described as an enclosed (or walled) garden, to be protected or penetrated. It has spring water and a fountain. The description is one of abundance, to compliment the sensory pleasures which arise from the relationship between the two lovers it also describes. Here is an orchard of pomegranates, herbs and aromatic plants such as cinnamon, henna and frankincense. The south wind is invoked with the hope it will blow the fragrance of its plants far and wide, a little like the effects of good love which has resonances far beyond the intimacy of a couple or a family.

During the pandemic, another large and interesting clergy garden grew in popularity as the Dean of Canterbury, Robert Willis, beamed Morning Prayer around the globe. Thousands watched and the animals in this contemporary Eden went viral. Tiger the cat enjoyed milk and pancakes on Shrove Tuesday. Dean Robert positioned himself amongst the collection of pigs, again all named, taking part of the service, at times in the pigsty. During Lent I wondered whether this had symbolic overtones of the ultimate story of shame and restoration—the Prodigal Son—the youngest son who squandered all his inheritance, mucking around humbly down with the pigs before returning to his father and childhood home. At a time of local as well as global challenge those who watched were invited to "stay awake", to accompany the dean in a vision of hope for the future, translated through an interpretation of the daily scripture readings. Not so different from that other famous biblical garden—Gethsemane—which has Jesus asking a group of faithful yet confused disciples to be alongside him at a troubled time.

Of course, it has long been recognized that gardening metaphors can be illuminating in terms of the inner spiritual journey in many religious traditions. Many sense that gardening is an active participation in the deepest mysteries of the universe. We talk about pruning to flourish more, in other words, sometimes hard, literally "cutting" experiences can, if we reflect enough, lead to a strange deepening as well as a broadening of who we are. It either makes us wither and die or expand in love. We can grow stronger but only with pruning from a wise gardener, whoever that might be for us. "Digging deep" is hard work but prepares the ground for a future. In other words, when we spend energy getting to know ourselves, dealing with the stones that need to be removed as well as feeding with nutrients, we tend to become people that others want to be around. Pruning, digging, planting, watering, fertilizing, abundance, beauty, sanctuary—all are here in Eden.

5

The habit of kindness

On my way to morning prayer, I stop off at the dry cleaners. The dry cleaners are not a business I regularly frequent, but today I am picking up a skirt which has had the zip mended at reduced rate rather than the full replacement. Jemima, the assistant there, has fixed it for me because she likes me. She likes me because I stopped to listen to her one day when she had been shouted at by an angry customer, insistent that some item of clothing was not ready, as promised. "I am still experiencing the trauma," she says, looking distressed. I take her hands and tell her I am so sorry for that. I have a daughter, waiting to begin her professional life as lawyer, who takes this kind of impatient nonsense on a daily basis as she works at a local food outlet. Now Jemima pauses, "You are a beautiful lady," she tells me. "I can tell," she shakes her head as I bat the compliment away. "Inside and out. You can tell, you know." She tells me more of her domestic woes, and she has clearly suffered. Injured people understand the power of simple, daily compassion, be it a word, a smile, some gentle, unelaborate graciousness offered without expectation of any transaction.

Those outside a church community often observe that the people within it are no better than those who do not frequent worship. There is sometimes truth in this but my experience over the years is that despite the mixed bags of who we all are trying to be, there is so much love shown. Phil, who has fixed my TV to the sitting room wall, jet washed my patio and repaired the washing machine, has done so all for the price of a bacon sandwich. He works (a retirement job) in a local supermarket, and he told me this story of contrasts. One morning he greeted a customer with "Good morning, madam. How are you?", to which she indignantly retorted, "What's that got to do with you?" Undeterred, he tried again with another. She replied, "Where shall I start?" In a quiet store, this warm-hearted man replied, "Try me." For the next 15 minutes, the woman poured out all her worldly troubles including an acute sense of desperate loneliness. But when she had finished, that sour wine had somehow turned into something better. The customer said, "Do you know, I feel brilliant now; I want to tell your manager about you." When the manager arrived, she told him that Phil had allowed her to just talk and, as shopping was scanned and packed, her day had found its colour and its hope again. A moment transformed by one kind question. A heart changed through the habit of kindness. Tiny but momentous, nevertheless. Parishioners who bring me small gifts when they know I am grieving on the death of my mother, flowers, samosas, cards. Kindness is like water these days. We must be vigilant to topping it up, in ourselves and in others who might be becoming dehydrated without it, traumatized, desperate, or lonely.

"She was kind to me," my best friend says, with tears in her eyes. As we sit in a chilly National Trust restaurant, that statement takes me aback, not only that she shows this unexpected emotion, but that she says this about my own mother. Not that my mother was not kind—she often was—but that this feature of her had affected my friend so deeply. "She introduced me to lentils," says Jacques, "and she worked hard to make sure we could still meet when you changed school. Without her I am not sure we would still be friends." My friend is right. Kindness could shape a life then, and these days, in our increasingly rushed and self-absorbed society, it feels a heightened spiritual value too—something which, if we can offer nothing else, can still be transformational. When genuinely offered, it inspires us to grow our own capacity for it too.

We get quite a few people through our church door who ask for money; it is the nature of the local area. Three mornings a week we offer hot drinks and toast and a face that hopefully smiles. This company offered by volunteers is that kindness, lived out tangibly even if it is "not enough". Even money, if it was offered, can be thrust upon someone unkindly and abruptly, an ambiguous offering which, ironically keeps people at arm's length to appease some kind of guilt. Kindness and the stuff that moves alongside it—gentleness, listening, patience—is longer lasting. It absorbs, like good perfume, into our skin and we remember its faint scent long after it has been applied.

As priest I am tuned to notice loneliness. You know an "alone" person who is unhappy with their solitude when they start talking to you even when you have done nothing to initiate a conversation. There are always two responses. You can brusquely or awkwardly ignore, or you can go with it, entering another's emotional space and diluting their sense of desolation. It is worth reflection—you might be the only person this stranger speaks to for the whole of the day, or week. I have a beautiful rug at home. Muted colours of mauve, camel, navy blue, teal; one half of it is still sharp with hue, the other drained from sun I am presuming. Kindness can do this; keep the colour sharp, keep the reason for being alive worth the trouble. Without it the intensity of life continuously unshared can burn away a little more of our capacity to bear it.

The world, thank God, is still full to the brim of inestimable kindness, which often feels like a gift of bountiful surprise when it arrives from the mouths or the hands of strangers. When we most need it, such kindness feels nothing short of miraculous. Jesus proved this to so many. As Christians we know the results of these divine acts of love but for many of us part of the power of kindness is that we do not know or see the results of what we do which sometimes have untold consequences. This is how Nick Cave puts it, "that what we do in this world means something; that we are not nothing; and that our most quotidian human actions by their nature burst the seams of our intent and spill meaningfully and radically through time and space, changing everything . . . Our deeds, no matter how insignificant they may feel, are replete with meaning, and of vast consequence, and . . . they constantly impact upon the unfolding story of the world, whether we know it or not."*

We are not impotent, he says, but instead we must come to terms with the fact that we are infinitely powerful and the way in which we conduct ourselves means a great deal. This tallies with what I believe. Sometimes I hate the pressure I put on myself or that others foist on me as holy person, that because I am priest, I can never be grumpy or rude or unfriendly. And when I am those things even with anonymous people, I feel uncomfortable and disappointed in my flinty, sometimes

---

* Maria Popova writing in *The Marginalian*, "Nick Cave and the antidote to our existential happiness".

lazy unkindness. So, my most consistent and urgent attitude is to carry this commitment to kindness always around with me, spreading it not cloyingly but lavishly particularly when the bread is dry and thin.

6

Valentine's Day

On my sitting room wall hangs a painting called *The Valentine*. It was painted by a Victorian artist called H.B (Henry Benjamin Roberts) and is of the sentimental genre subject matter the Victorian era cultivated so well—domestic scenes of family life. I would not necessarily have bought it, but Roberts happened to be my great great grandfather and the picture describes the playful exchange of a father teasing his daughter who has received a Valentine's card. He waves the unopened post aloft as his daughter, presumably desperate to read what is inside, reaches unsuccessfully for it. The scene depicts other family members who witness this scene and the artist leaves to the viewer's imagination what the conclusion might be.

I love the painting, proud to own such an heirloom and happy to tell the story of my rags-to-riches grandfather who, after an impoverished childhood, went on to do well, buying back many of his grandfather's paintings which had had to be sold so his mother and he could eat. Family, if it is happy and stable enough, models what good love looks like, as does this scene. It enjoys a moment, takes an interest in the private life of one of its members and does not take itself too seriously. It has always given me good vibes, an expression of wellbeing and belonging, a unit where identity and respect can be built, and like the relationship I had with my own grandparents, much mischievous fun which can strengthen and dissolve the tensions of a young life.

But in my own younger life, Valentine's Day always felt stressful. A potential desert of distress as no card or rose arrived from the person my body ached for. I had a childhood mostly inhabited by adults and until sixth form my education was at a girls' school. Although invited, I felt fear at belonging to the edgier crowd of girls who would go down to smoke and meet boys at the local coffee shop. I was shy around the

opposite sex and the times I did summon the courage to ask someone
out, that decision felt overly brave or unnaturally pushy, as I was rejected
or judged way too forward by slightly mystified young men.

Unlike my painting, the yearning for love and to be loved felt a long
way from light-hearted. It weighed heavy upon my own heart, as in my
young adulthood I realized I was ready for a relationship of significance
even though so often that seemed nowhere to be found. In my chosen
profession of clergydom, I worried I could not have both partner and
family as well as a vocation as a priest. Often troubled by concern that I
was threatening as a potential woman leader with my own strong will and
clear call, I feared I would be left on the proverbial shelf. Many of my male
fellow students seemed to be looking for old-fashioned vicar's wife-type
women who would happily settle in the domestic sphere, to raise children
and support the careers of their husbands. At that time in the Church
there seemed nowhere to go to even share that anxious discussion; no
older women of wisdom who would tell me that of course this was an
achievable and normal possibility. Many of these young men seemed to
feel threatened by a thinking woman who wanted to enter their domain,
and there was the matter of conflicting parishes and future callings. It all
seemed so complicated in my heart and mind. Needs are strong and love
grows darker the more unfulfilled it becomes.

Nowadays, although many remain frustrated at the continuous
irresolution of discussions regarding sexuality and its containment, there
at least feels to be some oxygen in terms of its discussion. And I for one
was lucky; I found my heart's desire, a line which runs through Psalm
21 and several others, in a gentle man who adored me and was not the
least bit threatened with my capabilities because he had enough of his
own. The enthusiasm I held for my calling was infectious it seemed, as
his own calling to be a priest built, and so began a parallel road.

Yet I still return to the loneliness I felt as a young adult. We can feel
most lonely when another's experience is filtered through our own
and can be accentuated when we are in a crowd. Most days I meet that
experience in others, it often hitting me like an unexpected splash of
water, draining the heart in a cold realization that someone is trying to
tell you their heart aches for some company or for another. Another who
has died, or left, or simply never been. Those encounters arrive within a

conversation about something utterly different, through the admittance of pain and the establishment of trust.

Thomas hangs around and seems not to want to leave. Have I time for a coffee? Of course, I say. We sit and talk about not very much as I scan the door, monitoring who is coming in. And Anna, her partner dead, the other members of her family seem not to bother to think that she might be alone at Christmas or on holiday. Gail Honeyman, in her novel about one lonely young woman, Eleanor Oliphant, writes:

> Loneliness is hallmarked by an intense desire to bring the experience to a close, something which cannot be achieved by sheer willpower or by simply getting out more, but only developing intimate connections. This is far easier said than done, especially for people whose loneliness arises from a state of loss or exile or prejudice, who have reason to fear or mistrust as well as long for the society of others.
>
> ... the lonelier a person gets, the less adept they become at navigating social currents. Loneliness grows around them, like mould or fur, a prophylactic that inhibits contact, no matter how badly contact is desired.*

For there is so much aching loneliness around and it seeps into a life. Clerics, like tired bath sponges, absorb so much of it. The priest's job is to hear this and to sense it, even when it remains unspecific. We must be kind even though we cannot stop every gap. But even five minutes of gentleness, of undistracted attention can feel like drops of relief on parched ground. We cannot make promises when we meet an insistence for reassurance. I counselled a young woman once whose husband discovered he was gay. That gentle emergence was a devastation for her as her hopes for a family and future with him fell like shattered glass through her dreams. Still married, she harangued me, seeking desperately an assurance that there would be another love. But I could not help, only share my own time of lonely misery and the belief that eventually we find

---

* Gail Honeyman, *Eleanor Oliphant Is Completely Fine* (London: HarperCollins, 2017), epigraph.

what we so passionately need in some form. Instead, clergy sit with others in their darknesses, however starved of love their own hearts might feel.

Over the years, I have listened to people tell me of the affairs they have had or are still having, unable to untangle the emotional mess they find themselves in. I have listened to those who yearn for sex after a lifetime of virginity, those with addictions to pornography, those who just want a friend or two, and to those who are so lonely that all I can do is wrap my priestly arms around them to tell them it is never too late to find love.

I have done Valentine's Day in church too, shaping the occasion to welcome back couples who have been married in the previous year as well as offering pastoral opportunities to celebrate the yearning to and for love in all the infinite varieties of partnerships. This feels so pressing in a post-Covid world, where isolation was felt so acutely by so many, like acid on a cut. Thankfully, my current congregation are a liberal bunch, many with queer or trans children who feel the silent judgment of an institution. Valentine's Day is problematic to the Church—a cultural event between Christmas and Easter—which it doesn't quite know what to do with, anxieties about providing a more wholesome and apparently redemptive antidote. Valentine's Day to the Church seems silently and patronizingly judged as shallow or somehow "not quite right", which I don't like that much, for underneath it all is our collective need to be held, and to be loved in all our oddness. If we got it right, perhaps 14 February just might become the opportunity for our deepest needs, our deepest damages to come out of hiding and to speak what we do not often have the courage to say, that we are mortal and fragile and know our need of love. In 2024, it fell on Ash Wednesday, perhaps the most symbolic of all days that emphasizes our earthly humanity.

We discover who we are and who we want to be through others and how they love us. We are remembered, as the old saying goes, not by our achievements but by the quality of relationships we create. The important thing in pastoral care is always how we leave another feeling, even if what they seek cannot be solved. People in a parish want many things of their priests, but really only one thing seems important—that their clergy love them, want to be with them, present in the ups and downs of their lives, trying to make sense of it all as people alongside. And to know in a place right down deep that whatever happens to them the love of a greater power is never transactional.

7

Hitching in South Africa

We had three weeks and not much money. I was 22 and spending the best part of a year in South Africa before apartheid finally fell to dust. Along with three companions I had made at the conference centre where I volunteered, we journeyed by coach to Cape Town. That time became one of the best adventures of my life, which included a few decisions of spontaneity emerging from the stupid courage of youth. One of my new friends was a young South African, and our actions for Will in particular proved sometimes hard to justify. Like all good pilgrimages, our journey involved stepping out of our comfort zones, packing lightly, being open to the kindness as well as the danger of strangers and the crossing of thresholds.

We arrived in Cape Town after a long bus ride and spent a few days in this energetic and cosmopolitan city. I bought some pink leather sandals in the market, listened to jazz musicians on the quay and escaped the resentful host who had had four young backpackers roll up to her small flat due to a tenuous connection of a friend of a friend back in the UK. As soon as she could, she dispensed with us, suggesting we stay in a relaxed and well-known district of Observatory. We spent one morning racing on the beach, the exhilaration of salty spray from the Cape's storm waves breaking all around us, whooping in the freedom only those on the cusp of adulting can feel. Robben Island glimpsed in the distance, a faint spot like the threat of a cancerous mole on the skin and not as yet a tourist destination. Another day was spent pulled up the mighty Table Mountain in a cable car, its flat top like a benign and respected uncle, its presence residing over the city beneath. Mist meant that, like that country's future, we could not see the panoramic, beautiful potential of the city beneath ripe for change.

I don't know whose decision it was to hitch all the way back to Melmoth, Natal—a journey of over a thousand miles. These days people do not seem to do this at all, the serial killer or malfunctioning stranger lurking in conventionally safe places but mostly deep within our imaginations. Hitching is hard work, especially in the heat, and back then it required immense patience and a philosophical approach. Exasperation at the drive-pasts and growing desperation need to be thrown out of the window like discarded rubbish as our own water bottles emptied. To successfully hitch, you need to be at the edges of anywhere. In the city centre, drivers tend to just want to get out and drive home. To practise the art well, the hitcher needs to think their way into making it easy for someone to stop. Hard shoulders, lay-bys, places to slow down are positions well-chosen and where an adventure began. The unpredictability of what we were doing felt edgy, dangerous, and full of possibility. Perhaps the giving up of the usual comforts which more conventional travellers have is worth it for momentary and spontaneous new encounters and the wind in your hair. Townships in South Africa are always on the edge of main conurbations or else outside of them completely. Traveller communities often site themselves in car parks on the edge of town.

In the volatile country which South Africa was at the time, where anyone could carry arms and there seemed so much anger around, doing this was crazily dangerous. Continuous eruptions of violence were everywhere, and although Will was with us, we stood out like sore British thumbs every time we opened our mouths. So, we stood, ever hopeful, in the blistering heat, rucksacks chaffing bare shoulders, waiting for any vehicle to stop. We longed, after a desperate hour, to cross the threshold of any vehicle going anywhere out of the city. We often stood in what felt like a liminal no-man's-land, vast and derelict spaces of dust, the opposite of places with names and addresses, neighbours and boundaries.

Rioting in the townships meant we could not go to some of these, although for several of our trips we ventured into the taxi ranks, where only black and local people travelled. A chaos of minibuses with no seeming order to the destination, we discovered them simply by asking. Once found and paid for, we crammed ourselves in, fielding the mystified glances of those who wondered why white youth were daring to travel in such a way, and waited until the stuffy and unbearably hot tin box was full enough to begin its journey. We travelled by taxi when there really seemed no other option for this meant spending the little money we had, sharing with feathers and livestock as well as humanity.

On the major routes, black, brown and white people all stopped. We got a lift with a businessman in a Merc who just liked the company, a local woman picking up her kids from school, workmen in the cabin of a bulldozer (slow going), and in several windswept backs of trucks. Several of the lift-givers also offered us accommodation for the night—potentially dangerous, but luckily for us, simply a natural and kindly desire to help young people, reminding them of the vulnerability of their own kids, off living somewhere in another place. One man offered his caravan in the garden, and he and his wife fed all four of us dinner, sharing their opinion of where they believed their country was headed. Cathartic to have willing recipients to foist anxiety upon, or genuinely interested in the far-away perspective brought near in this opportune encounter. Another dropped us off at our planned youth hostel but invited us to a family party which was happening the same evening; we were the only white people there and were welcomed and fed magnificently. We stayed with a much-loved priest on the edge of Lesotho who did not agree with women in holy orders and told me so from the outset. But Fr Martin's hospitable benevolence was like no other and came as a welcome respite after the hardness of busy youth hostels and attitudes of antagonism from others. We had been subjected to this in the hills, staying at a pizza restaurant owned by a biased and angry relative of Will who clearly did not like Brits or their opinions of his country. I grew sick of pizza quite quickly and our host's constant fight-picking belligerence. But the variety of people whom we encountered exemplified my growing understanding that this nation was truly like a rainbow, multi-faceted and complex.

Hitching meant that our destinations were often unpredictable, as we were sometimes dropped off in places which inevitably suited the drivers more than it did us. In an age before the safe dependency of the mobile phone, there was no way to communicate with our fellow traveller-pair (we often hitched in a male–female combo for safety); we simply trusted that at some point we would meet in the recommended place and mostly we did.

Ministry requires much generosity of spirit as clerics are called to think the best of people and to trust more than to be suspicious—a tall order in the damp and claustrophobic age of uber-carefulness and risk assessment. That three-week adventure of hitchhiking taught me that mostly the risk is worth it, the jeopardy of stepping into other's spaces and hearts, never taking for granted the kindness of others as well as giving others benefit of the doubt. On that South African adventure there was only one moment when I felt genuine danger. Two of us (strangely the only day I and the other girl had decided to hitch together) were picked up by a van with an open back. There were several young lads who drove us into the middle of nowhere and asked us if we wanted to go back to their home. I smelt danger then and adamantly insisted we were taken to a place on a main road where we could continue the journey on our own.

But it is also on the edges where vulnerability can be turned into something transformative. There is freedom to respond well at the edge it feels, perhaps because there is less to lose. Mark Boyle, a former businessman who lived without money for three years and now lives in Ireland in a tech-free existence, tells this beautiful story. Once when he himself was hitching, he realized he had left his only, freshly filled water bottle behind in a car. Without it he would have been forced to search for an empty bottle and find a toilet to fill it from (not having or being able to use any money to buy a new one). But one hour and one hitch later, the man in whose car Boyle had left the water bottle pulled up. He had spent 40 minutes searching for this hitchhiker, realizing how important the bottle would be to him, having heard the rationale of his moneyless life. The man then shared that he had been in prison for two years after a fight in a night club. "Here he was, going to all lengths to make sure a complete stranger had his water bottle." It reinforced Boyle's belief that "there is no such thing as a 'good' or 'bad' person; each of us is just as capable of huge acts of kindness and generosity as we are of causing harm."* That story reminded me that human beings have a great propensity to dig deep and to search for any connections they might have with someone else to establish a relationship. It happened in the various vehicles I travelled in in South Africa too and was part of the pilgrimage I took to grow into the faith that was being shaped within my life.

---

*   Mark Boyle, *The Moneyless Man: A Year of Freeconomic Living* (Oxford: Oneworld, 2019).

8

Urban pilgrim

Half past two on a cloudy Friday afternoon I wanted a change of scene after a funeral for a despondent and tiny congregation. I took off to explore the city's waterways by bike. The concept of pilgrimage is current and sharp, like the wind that penetrated the hidden warmth of my body, layered with waterproofs. True pilgrims travel light, so I took coat, door keys, phone and water with me. My starting point was a historic mill, the cycle route emerging easily into a field, weaving alongside the River Cole, polluted and poorly snake—rubbish its food, chucked unkindly into its feeble trickle; it seemed to mirror the poverty encountered on my journey at every turn. And this was not the insufficiency of things but poverty as a lumped accumulation of all that is not needed, a thoughtless dispensing, thrown over a boundary of what we consider to be ours alone. I felt sorry for the river, as I did for those who were responsible for its sickness. Sorry for their unawareness of what every act of sabotage this dumping does to the wildlife and general aesthetic of the city and the effect on innocent walkers and cyclists out for an attempt at fresh air in this urban place. It felt like an ailing animal, unable to get better and flourish, perpetually being fed the wrong food.

I crossed roads and confronted the vibrancy of a huge fruit stall, found the path again, cycled behind old brick factories, at the back of gardens whose boundaries were nothing more than a line of zigzag bent corrugated iron sheets with yet more rubbish piled up. Emerging onto an industrial site and skirting the outskirts of a dry ski slope where teenagers on half term were whooping down in large rubber rings, I needed to find the canal.

In her book *The Soul of a Pilgrim*, Christine Valters Paintner quotes this distinction, "To journey without being changed is to be a nomad. To change without journeying is to be a chameleon. To journey and be transformed by the journey is to be a pilgrim."* Travelling is like this too. Organized holidays—tours—tend to concentrate on the brushed-up sides of any given place, the dirty and problematic parts conveniently set aside, airbrushed out of any itinerary. But genuine travel does what the quote says, it gets into your blood, as the unpleasant smells, legacies of past exploitation are trodden into the very ground—sights of children in rags or blown off limbs—that is what changes you.

I find myself here in this city having come full circle—I am back after 20 years living elsewhere. Never for a minute I imagined I would return to a place I had previously become bored with, like a spoilt and insatiable traveller, always demanding new horizons constantly. But I have been surprised by feelings of fond familiarity. It is, I know, a mending time after trauma. For I am bewildered by an overwhelming sense of return, of "coming home", to this startling city of many colours and many faiths. Before when all was new for me, the inspiration of such a diverse and invigorating place, provocative and fresh—this is the city I trained in, got married and had my children. And those early days of life, as my own maturity emerged, were happy. Now, a new consciousness merges with those memories, as clouds at different levels of sky morph into one mass, creating a present of sharp expectancy and hope.

This afternoon I am not priest; I am simply me, could be anyone, out for air and adventure on my bike. I pass it all, the back of a decorated warehouse wall, where pumping music warms the walls. I walk past the back of higher education colleges, their lunchtime tables ghostly and uninhabited in reading week. I pass few people, a Muslim mum in a burka with two lively children in tow, a dog walker and woman so grey with a sense of bleak life her depression seems clear without her even speaking.

This pilgrimage is different to those from my childhood. One, a windy trudge to the half-buried Oratory of St Piran, patron saint of Cornwall, along the vast expanse of Perranporth Beach, named after this saint. It is one of Britain's oldest Christian sites from the sixth century. The chapel remained in use probably until the tenth century and through the centuries has been buried by sand and then excavated again. I remember

---

*   Christine Valters Paintner, *The Soul of a Pilgrim* (Notre Dame, IN: Sorin Books, 2015), p. 1, quoting Mark Nepo from *The Exquisite Risk*.

it being half submerged and this fact alone provided a sense, throughout my young life, of a fascination for places or treasure which had been submerged. These small adventures gave me a taste for quirky places— buildings, woods, and follies, places which had absorbed a tacit sense of mystery and sometimes creepiness. Places of implicit holiness as well as haven, like Lud's Church, a deep mossy chasm created by a massive landslip in the hillside above Gradbach in Cheshire, associated with the secret hiding and worship place, safe from the persecutions of the age, of John Wycliffe and his followers in the fourteenth century.

My parents too had a taste for visiting less well-known spots associated with the building of community, Sempringham in Lincolnshire and Rosslyn in Scotland, the latter now made famous from Dan Brown's infamous novel, *The Da Vinci Code*. Then my parents were concerned not with the chapel's incredible stonework but with the humble vision of service begun by Roland Walls, courageous and visionary priest who founded the Community of the Transfiguration, a group of people who opted out of conventional life to one instead of voluntary poverty and the discipline of prayer. I experienced first-hand their permanently open table, munching dry sandwiches filled with peanut butter in a green corrugated hut, at a lunch open to those visiting, sitting alongside those who, unkempt and smelly, were as welcomed as we were.

But today I call myself an urban pilgrim, for where I go is both familiar as well as new. The landscapes of my memory are overlaid with what has sprung up—areas revitalized and rebuilt and yet still so much muck, hardy swans competing with various items of floating plastic. I pass dog shit piles, discarded mattresses, dirty clothes, thrown food containers— the detritus of our bodies and their needs. This area—Bordesley and Digbeth—is heavily graffitied in signatures which pulsate with garish colour and a deep desire to make one's mark. A flamboyant language devised by rebellious tribes, who like nomads, feel as though they cannot fit, nor want to ascribe to conventions which hem them in. These are bold and indecipherable statements, hunted out blank canvases in hidden places where this culture is expressed magnificently. I have always loved graffiti and its outdoor glory.

I peddle on, through several long and frightening tunnels, the stuff of horror films. These are lit at least, but I feel overly close to the oily, greenish water, the ancient bricks above me sugary with dust and salt and cobwebs. Dark and claustrophobic spaces have always frightened me, murky waters too. A couple of these tunnels feel older, more historic and instantly I feel happier, a familiar feeling of heritage, the reassurance of the National Trust somewhere nearby. In two of these tunnels, I am forced to dismount—I cannot go as fast as I might like. But this is the nature of pilgrimage. Pace is dictated by the journey, to realize you are not in control, allowing time to respond to all encountered along the way, to the weather, to getting lost or exhausted, to the unexpected, as here. A good pilgrimage takes as long as it takes, allowing the momentum to find its own rhythm. All of this happened to me that afternoon. An assumption of what might have been a quick half an hour took two and a half instead. I kept stopping, taking snaps of what caught my eye. I got lost in the moment and at the junction where I knew I needed to change canal towpaths when I just could not work out where I needed to go. It got colder and I was thirsty, beginning to yearn for the warmth of home and a hot drink. I neared the city centre and felt more comfortable, less lonely. Here were tall buildings, new, glistening in purple glass. The city was on the cusp of coming alive for the night, the bars ready for the influx of exhaustion and binge drinking after a working week. By then I was long gone from the canal basin, which was both familiar and yet unrecognizable to me, like a long-lost friend you meet again of which there have been a few on my return into this city.

Tomorrow is Palm Sunday, the beginning of the most significant of weeks for those who want to really feel the complete experience Christ took to the cross. We start our local pilgrimage at one of the churches in my parish and end up at the other. A giant cross will stand in the middle of "the green", an outdated description which has stuck, leftover association of what used to be a genuine village. This green is still the centre of the area, a place where those with nothing and no one to fill their time sit, with their cans of Monster and Special Brew, smoking their joints in their feisty trainers. They shout at one another and passers-by just as they did at Jesus as he sat, stolidly on the donkey on that day thousands of years ago.

I will stand with my congregation, on a typical March day, harsh breeze and playful sun darting between clouds. Coffee shops opening, people on their way to somewhere far more exciting than an outdoor church service of sorts. Yet this strange ritual of placing the cross in the middle of our concrete green is still appreciated, noticed. It speaks of an unspoken comfort in a season which still retains strangely, a significance of sorts, new life possibility, a yearned for hope, or simply a meal of spring lamb shared with friends. And, once the story of Jesus on trial (traditional on this day) is acted out by members of the church, we walk now, a coy publicity of faith, through the streets, past the homeless outside the Co-op, past the bus stops, past the vomit and rubbish from the night's revelries, to our other building where a small but beautifully faithful few are gathered, the band of current living saints. Most of us carry that tightness of embarrassment, participating in the oddness of all this which seems either fascinating or anathema to those who watch. I hand out crosses to whoever will accept them.

Pilgrimage implies personal quest, some kind of "walking out" through walking short or long distances. We walk to discover a sense of who we are, we walk to let down the irritant and scarred parts of the past. Sometimes that is a vain hope for it is more than possible to walk a very long way without thinking too much or too deeply. But for others, catharsis grows and lodges, as a pilgrim's future surfaces. That happened to me at university, when lonely and bewildered a regular pilgrimage was made by bus into Coventry, a city permanently and triumphantly grey, as I found my way to the cathedrals. Juxtaposed next to one another, there is the natural and symbolic progression of obliteration to renewal, as the shell of the old cathedral bombed so catastrophically in the Second World War leads to the spiky yet now dated bold newer building. Here, I walked back into my faith again as I circled the building's interior often, its strange tapestry of Sutherland's gigantic Christ, other art and its defiant statements of vision through a purged reconciliation. I found there a peace and way forward, an acceptance that what is past is always partly good and cannot be completely dispensed with. My love of divine life and helping others to sense that was shaped, strained over those few months. And to arrive there, something of an end to my pilgrimage at that stage, meant leaving a sense of the precipitous void of the unknown and the unhappy. Those pilgrimages took me beyond a preoccupation with myself into the taste for a more expansive adventure.

9

Can I talk to you?

Jonathan has something about him. It cannot be defined, but I recognize a distinctive and delicate focus within another which makes me simply want to spend time in his presence. Some kind of strange holiness? But no one feels "holy" and shouldn't either. That idea either makes people laugh or else it places a heavy sense of expectation on how someone chooses to live. But over the years people like him have found a place in my life's landscape. To define the quality which is generic amongst such people would be to drain it of its mystery, for everyone is different. Yet there is maybe something about the well of silence carried in the depths of a person, which others can dip and drink from. I am led to become more silent in such a presence, the torrent of thoughts and deluge of words in head and heart naturally wanting to wilt. I have sensed it in certain individuals where there resides a kind of purity, whilst in others it is an untold yet integrated suffering. Jonathan possesses an aura; he wears an invisible cloak of calm. And there feels a stationary safety—of non-judgment and an openness to anything I might bring. Knowing people like him feels like discovering gold as you pan the friends and colleagues of your life and spot the ones that strangely gleam. These gleamers are often people who spend serious time practising meditation or prayer or just seem to possess a natural quiescence. They are unafraid of silence and indeed may seek it out within the turbulence of life.

I do not for one moment put myself in this category, but I have found myself in the last few years in a place where an eclectic group of people seem to want to talk to me. I am a strange breed in the world, one named spiritual director or more commonly now perhaps the softer spiritual guide or accompanier for we do not take so much to being directed in our current age. Sitting and listening alongside another as they work out how a sense of the divine might be speaking within their inner life is what these times are about. There is an art to allowing the right questions to be asked and the right answers to emerge. Or to allow the questions to remain but perhaps to understand them from a new place. There can be too, the spilling out of a long-carried secret, the heavy damage of life's terribleness, infidelity, unhappiness, rape, illness, abuse which cannot be defined or named, or the weight of what is so often now a life of pressure. It can be uncomfortable, costly and exhausting work but also a role which is deeply satisfying.

Spiritual guiding is different from counselling or psychotherapy. It does not seek to fix or cure through a certified discipline. It has affinities to these practices yes, as well as to life coaching and our contemporary interest in wellbeing. Although people undertake a course of training, it is still distinctively different from these other forms of helping. Different because it relies on a deep well of listening space from one person and the reliance on the power of a third presence (I name as the Holy Spirit or divine power) to lead the conversation into where it needs to go.

Priests are people of words, and if we are good priests, we use them with care. There is nothing worse than a cleric who talks too much, dominates the conversation with over enthusiasm or ego, flattening any chance of the smaller glimmers of insight from another to break in. But words are everywhere. Ben Okri says that our days in this age seem often poisoned with too many words, words said and not meant, and words said *and* meant. Words can wound and hide and diminish. Opinions which bombard. For me there are sometimes simply just too many words, even in church. Is there a kind of "too muchness"—even of rich and thoughtful words—like some kind of perpetual verbal banquet we have the opportunity of swallowing at every moment?

We need spiritual spaces where words do not rip and damage. Places where we do not leave exhausted by soapbox rants or emotional need expressed in verbal overflow. We need spaces to tell our stories and to listen to the stories of others, which land in our imaginations and begin to take root in soil where dreaming and connection happens, stories which grow our lives because they resonate with something we know to be true. We need spaces where silence is offered because the invisible power of it has been trusted for centuries, the effects of it like nothing else for it allows us to sink into rest as well as acceptance. Silence does not necessarily mean a lack of words, for the stopping of exterior verbalization often means that the conversation continues in our heads instead. Real silence means a shutting down of this mental chatter for a time.

My own spiritual guide gave me a Rumi poem recently, set within an article on an understanding of poetry. It proved timely for me, a mysterious offering—why this piece of writing at this moment, which echoed so much with a particular internal struggle which was happening on the nature of suffering. It has been read, re-read, mentally chewed over as well as shared with others and so the spiritual wisdom embeds and is passed on. The poem is only a few lines long, but it holds a truth and a dignity and had become a doorway through which to move away from a place of pain and into a new room where that suffering feels a little lessened. That is what spiritual direction is about. A sensing of where someone is up to and what they might need.

The world needs more of this quiet wisdom. It needs less gossip, interruption, opinionated and one-sided shoutings which are hurled into our lives like bricks, with not much thought for where or how these will land to those on the receiving end. It needs voices which are measured and soothing, voices which can tell universal stories. It needs eyes which can look into the eyes of another head on, without flinching or embarrassment. We enter such an understanding with trepidation either as recipient or as guide. As recipient because it can feel alarming, destabilizing to have someone observe elements about us that we might or might not see and even if we do, can sometimes not really admit. And as a guide because we feel the pressure to say and offer the exact pertinent thing, without further wounding or challenge which is not asked for. We tiptoe on the shards of the soul as we weigh up words or stories which are being yearned for from another. Being a guide is like being a good parent or grandparent, guardians who watch but with a respectful spaciousness for the other person to unfold a little more. Watch closely lest those in your care hurt themselves but do not hold too tight in case you waste your energy being drawn into another's world of high octane and emotion. There is always holiness in risk. That even when challenge is needed it is accepted only because it has been asked for. And after there has been a fall then we often need help to make sense of the things which trouble, the questions all of us hold as we walk around our lives.

Spiritual direction is not something reserved for people who are "religious". It is for anyone who senses some "other-ness" about their own lives and about life generally. It is for those who naturally understand that all that which is commonplace and ordinary can be infused with the spiritual—that we walk on holy ground all the time. Working out our own place to that is what it is about. Priests often make good spiritual guides because they are somehow expected to be. In popular consciousness they are still people with time on their hands to develop such practices and have been trained to ruminate on all that seems beyond, numinous and unexplained as well as earthed and sore.

This perception is no bad thing but those of us who wear this identity badge have to be ready to do it well for it feels an opportunity to offer something lifegiving in an often cynical and desolate world. But this is also essentially an everyday activity as well as something which is specially arranged. For many conversations arise in the street, sharing meals, in the school corridor, at the bus stop and especially in the pub. Any sincere chat about God and the meaning of life and love is what I understand to be "spiritual guiding". The Desert Fathers and Mothers of the third century who lived as hermits and ascetics in Egypt often used very prosaic examples (being alone, bread, laughter, death) to teach wisdom, often seeking one another out as spiritual guides.

I have had a number of spiritual guides over the years—all kind, wise and soaked in life experience. Some men and some women, the right people at the right time. They are often also just people I respect and enjoy being in the company of. A good guide knows when to affirm and soothe but also when to challenge, always gently. People often rich in stories and anecdotes, their offerings can be taken as substantial bread or left as crumbs if this does not help. My own guides have asked "What is saving your life right now?"—a question which has reconnected me with joy in its most profound understanding. What is worked on between two people who become conduits of God for one another, holds the most amazing and growing vitality.

1 0

Confession

A month of growth is March. Winds blow in change and a carnival of flowers. The freshness of spring pushes into the tense and ungrateful worlds we create around ourselves. Who doesn't love a snowdrop, their squat bells laughing at the ridiculousness of the world, as they, in their fragile resilience break through the hardest of ground? Crocuses, purple-thin pencils trampled on as soon as they have emerged, by runaway footballs and small children escaping the confines of parents on a windy day in a litter strewn park. Growth happens despite us but also at strange moments, invading periods of our lives where we do not expect it. Sometime later we notice there has been a change within us, a stretching, parts of us painted over, like a wall we walk past every day which has had a fresh wash of colour. And like those walls, we become aware that something feels different and there has been a shift away from the "us" to which we are familiar.

Growth happens too when we heal from past failures, when transformation falls like a voile on things we finally find the courage to look at, hidden in the background of who we are. The concept of being sorry and of being forgiven is the stuff of much Christian-speak. Each Sunday those who gather in church say what is known as "the confession". We say this collectively, a nod to the fact that every human person fails and contains fragilities as well as the fact that we are all bound up in practices and global economies that we can never gain complete control of. Dynamics which inevitably connect us with the problems of eternity—slavery, planet-misuse and violence of investing in shoddy work practice. Now we have to think every time we eat a piece of tropical fruit. This is corporate sin, a word we don't much like these days, at least in the faith circles I move in. We are discouraged to use the word in schools (or anywhere unless it refers to something banal like eating chocolate cake) lest it encourage an unhealthy sense of guilt, deemed as abusive or encouraging a degraded sense of self-worth. We automatically absorb this age-old story from Genesis, the first book in the Bible, where Adam and Eve disobey God and eat the fruit of the forbidden tree of knowledge. Their mistake, in Eden, to compete with God because of it.

I like the idea of taking some responsibility for structural sin, of understanding that I am connected with many others who might not have such a great life because of the choices I have or am making in the here and now. Through confession then, I can wipe the slate clean regularly, as many modern mindfulness and meditation exercises help us to do, as well as prayers from other faith traditions. This feels healthier than the sense that we as individuals have to bear the weight of our own dirty and secret faults. But this collective reciting of communal confession has occasionally too, felt a slight abnegation of responsibility, that because everyone says it, all of us have sinned in the same way and are bound up in a bland understanding of corporate misdoing, an eternal Ferris wheel of vague naughtiness. In a moment, the experience is over, however sincerely we have engaged with the words. Often, I feel unready, and I wonder, whether others share a feeling that personal behaviours take much effort to change, but remain unresolved and uncomfortable, swept, like gritty dirt under the carpet.

But an understanding of "sin" in terms of doing something wrong is still evident in our collective consciousness. We just have different words for it now which somehow feel harsher and more potent—"abuse" and "misconduct" being two of them. The experience of judging and being judged is sharper and more public than ever. We tut and shake our heads when someone in public life falls from grace, most of us secretly grateful it was not us who was caught with our pants down or hands in the till.

Around the age of seven, I was taken to confession. Looking back, it seems a strange thing to suggest to a child. But I understand it was about the practising of what was perceived then to be a healthy habit like prayers before bedtime and eating your greens. Kneeling before the tall and willowy figure of Fr Catling, with his hooked nose, my hands gripped the shiny communion rail, as I desperately tried to remember something I had done wrong and was genuinely sorry for. Goodness knows what that solemn but kindly priest thought of my spilled-out apologies of tiny acts of selfishness and stolen sweets. But I remembered he always listened graciously and intently and then, in a grave voice, would offer me small pieces of advice about how to approach my young life. I cannot remember what these might have been now, but my mother considered him a saintly man. The experience, which would happen about three or four times every year, did not damage, but it was something I decisively decided not to inflict upon my own children. Attitudes and ways of dealing with wrongdoing move on.

Yet the practice of confession is also far from dead or irrelevant. For whatever our beliefs most of us have an inbuilt moral code of how to behave, of how to treat others, even if we live through periods when we become careless with that code. We instinctively understand we cannot be selfish or rude. That we should care for and help others, contribute to society appropriately within our means and capabilities, or if none of these, then at least we understand that we should not break the law. There have been a few distinctive times when I have sought out someone to talk to, about a growing and overwhelming sense of wanting to say sorry for something. Times in my life when there has been a sense of being caught, trapped, in some kind of strange behavioural rut, resulting in a feeling of soul-desolation.

Alongside this there have been distinctive occasions when I have felt the need to change unhealthy habits which have created a sense of life becoming sullied and heavy. Specific occasions when I have felt the insistent urge to seek another out for what might be described as a "confession". Times when I have felt in need of the wise counsel and soothing spirit of a perceived holy person, someone who would, yes understand, but also offer me some positive way out which would dilute a burden of shame. There is a way of offering wisdom like this and I still feel privileged when others regard me as such a person. It is to do with a sense of utter acceptance, philosophical attitude and the ability to "turn around" how that person is viewing who they have become. Confession is not a simple "fessing up", a claiming of responsibility for wrongdoing, although it is sometimes. It is often an acknowledgment that you have somehow squandered a bit of your life, and that although you could have sworn you knew which way you were headed, you have lost sight of the path that you thought you would never leave. Sometimes it is the feeling of some kind of strange defilement, that our life, or a part of it, has become tarnished with something that does not feel right or at least right with who we think we are trying to be.

The first time I sought confession was as a sixth-former. My father had just died, and I cherished an insistent flame for my art teacher who personified the gentle, paternal figure I had lost. As the feeling of fondness grew, so much so that it became unbearable—the archetypical crush—I reached a point where I did not know what to do with it, a bomb of pent-up love I wanted to dispense with lest it blew up at the wrong moment. I sought out the school chaplain and dumped it all at his shiny feet. He was, I recall, magnificent in his balancing of empathetic understanding of where I was at in terms of bereavement as well as sexual awakening.

The second time was after I had done something unthinkable as an ordinand. I had fallen pregnant while having a relationship with another student. Feeling instinctively that I was not ready to have a child, and that the relationship was not right for us at that time, I had a termination. To this day I believe that decision was the right one for the future I was to lead, but it did not stop me feeling shame, partly because of the secret nature of what I decided to do. My friends were supportive, but I was too frightened of the consequences of what might happen if I told my tutors at my college or my family. I was fairly sure I would have been asked to leave, and having worked so hard to get to where I was, I could not contemplate that possibility. The thought of being judged harshly by my mother was also unbearable, for I was already judging myself because of that secret act.

Some months later I went to stay at a convent for a bit of quiet and space. Those of us in professional religious life call this "a retreat". I sought out a nun to talk to, as often this opportunity is offered, hoping, in some twisted way, that she would chastise me for what I had done or anaemically absolve me of the impossible sense of shame I carried. Here was not official confession but what happened was indeed an absolution, a sense of being freed from the trap I had constructed for myself. My understanding up to that point was that abortion was always wrong; it was a kind of killing of life, iincomprehensible for someone training to be professionally holy. Or it was the stuff of ethical discussion, a subject clinically debated from an often-moral theological high ground, without any awareness that it might have happened to someone in the room. But my nun's response after the "confession" was to remind me of all the thousands, millions even, of sperm in one act of sex. It proved the most intensely helpful image and an incredibly kind way of releasing me from the shame that burned in me every day. Effectively she was asking me to alter my perception of myself and what had happened which had been fed to me by religious conservatives, that every life was precious and to be honoured and that I was wicked. Every life *is* precious, but that nun reminded me that at that stage, within my own body, that tiny miracle of life beginning was a very long way from what we might understand to be a person. I cannot remember whether she forgave me in any official capacity, through some kind of liturgical rite. All I knew was that I somehow had to lay the experience to rest, or at least to find a box to put it in safely. A place where it could travel with me to become a positive piece of the toolkit in the help and kindness offered to others in the future. But the encounter I had with that sister whose name I cannot remember progressed my own healing and became a conversation I will never forget.

There are moments in a life when we know we should confess something but do not or cannot bring ourselves to do it. And there are times when we do confess things that we probably do not need to. But whatever position we take often unexpected grace is received as well as wise love from those we least expect. Real confession is when we seriously "take counsel", when we are ready to say it as it really is, when we are truly prepared to be utterly honest about how we have messed up, transgressed or regressed, honest enough to stop being the victim, to stop making excuses for our lack of discipline, diving far down through the mired layers of ourselves to find a new clarity in our own depths.

Through the years, a priest finds unlikely as well as unexpected people seeking confession. And in my denomination, they often do not come into a shadowed church, full of flickering candles, to a cassock-clad cleric and before a grill which disguises identity. They come for a coffee, to my home, or I to theirs, and often small talk comes first, a testing out of whether the courage can be found to divulge the secret or set down the burden. A man with a problem with gambling, a woman who used to steal. The man nearing the end of his life who had never told his wife he had had an affair when in the navy and felt deeply guilty. Another who has never told anyone what they end up telling me. Clergy are chosen often because of their traditional status to be able to absolve and forgive, sometimes chosen because it is believed the skeleton in someone's closet can remain buried but with the bones put to rest. Or chosen because of a perceived ability to listen and absorb tricky or controversial subjects, people who can help ease the bump when the load is thrown down, someone who can rearrange that load with a bit more arrangement for the way ahead. Or simply to help with closure. And there is a holiness as well as a privilege in all of that, the fact that people are prepared to speak the unspeakable and seek release in the company of another who is trusted.

The truth is that we cannot heal from what we cannot acknowledge. And we cannot absolve that which is not sincerely offered for it is about the state of another's heart. But when our heart has not caught up with our head this does not work in the end. It is akin to the insisted apology one child must make to another, without each party really owning responsibility. When we present our exhausted selves, sometimes just seeing the goodness, wisdom or philosophy radiating from another is all we need for it to be restored within ourselves. As Augustine says, "Who can be good, if not made so by loving?" And that is right, for restoration happens when we are loved and listened back to a place of mending by those who we instinctively trust to deliver it.

1 1

Sisters, saints and silence

There is both a refreshment as well as a discomfort in silence. I sat in the cool room with high windows alongside my grandmother, chairs spaced carefully in a circle. I was the only child present. As the daughter of a clergyman, I was used to breathing the air of stilled sanctity and knowing when I should not speak. This occasion held the familiarity of a church service as well as feeling distinctive, different—there being the kind of peace which descends in a kitchen where the cook is absorbed shelling peas or beans. A hush where inner worlds are unlocked through a secure domesticity, where the absence of words sustains as well as mends and all is done gently. Here was a room of understood tranquillity, when silence descends like the scented air on a late summer evening and the birds understand it is time to stop their chirping.

One woman stood up. She shared her impression of me arriving to the "Meeting" that morning, my full scarlet skirt of red cotton reminding her of the beauty of a field of poppies and the hope those flowers herald. It was a lovely image and a surreptitious way of including me in a world which might have felt temporarily strange to a child. What she said has stayed with me, more than I can say for hundreds of sermons I have listened to over the years. I liked the way people only shared when they felt inspired by something within them. It felt a more careful, reverent way of choosing words, of relishing them and making them holy. And all had permission to do so.

My grandparents were Quakers. Somehow the quietness of its practice seemed akin to the placid person my grandmother was. Renowned for their inclusive approach to all faiths, as a Quaker she seemed similarly devoid of any judgment of others. I never heard her raise her voice or say an unkind word about anyone save for the briefest of irritations.

Throughout the Second World War her house became a shared haven from Jewish doctors to American soldiers billeted on the family because they lived near to the South Coast. My mother slept on a camp bed for years, but the rewards were fantastic sugary treats showered upon her by young Yanks missing their own kids.

I have inherited my grandmother's bureau. It is a marvellous space-saving piece of furniture, made of oak, so it takes the removal men by surprise when they come to lift it. It has shelves and a fold-down desk section, small drawers for keeping stationery and secret treasures. I remember her so often sitting there, her back to me, writing a cheque for some charity rep who had arrived at the door. The amount was always £5.00—far more than this feels today—and she had a small notebook where she kept a record of all she gave.

Silence has always been important and necessary to me too. I love its balm after hours of good conversation with my friends. Its substance is like no other, like the feeling of silk on your skin. I had a friend a while back who was also a member of the "Society of Friends" as Quakers are also known. That feels a loving and inclusive title for a spiritual community. My friend had a Quaker wedding, and it was beautiful. The couple stood up at an appropriate moment and declared their love and commitment to one another. Other friends and family, out of that silent serenity, celebrated by rising to stand, sharing a selection of recollections and good wishes.

Throughout my life I have enjoyed times when the lives and spiritual traditions of those closest to me have moved alongside my own. I married a Moravian, and that pietist religious denomination expanded my knowledge and fed me in ways my own did not. Moravians are a European Protestant denomination, who, although they have bishops as leaders, are a far more egalitarian group, calling each other, whoever you are, "brother" and "sister". When they die, everyone has the same sized gravestone and to wander around God's Acre is an experience which prompts questions of how humanity so quickly builds inequalities. Theirs was a mission-oriented church, and the Moravians still enjoy lively communities in the Caribbean, Tanzania and elsewhere; my husband was born in Jamaica for example. In this country they are famous for creating "settlements", which, although still lived in, are often used as film sets, as they are ready made villages of old-fashioned history with their cobbled streets and unaltered community buildings. I inherited a wonderful set of friends from my husband, one a minister. Occasionally I have participated in their monthly sharing of bread and wine, described as a Love Feast with Holy Communion. Their Watch Night service is famous as it heralds in the New Year, and the tradition of Christingle, now celebrated in many churches, originated with the Moravians. Their non-hierarchical approach to faith, to God, appeals to me, their congregations gathered in contrast to the idea that as a parish priest there is an exhausting obligation to be responsible for all who reside there.

My mother, disillusioned with what she perceived to be the lack of depth in Anglican spirituality, became interested in the Orthodox tradition, and along with an unconventional priest working with people who are mentally vulnerable founded Cornwall's first Orthodox church in a quiet, creek-filled backwater of the town where we lived. Over the years I accompanied her to worship in various parts of the country, often tiny, cramped spaces, walls lined with glossy icons and heavy with incense. There is a sensuality to Orthodox worship; you kiss icons, honour God by bowing right to the floor, and chant much of the service. Children unintentionally absorb its rituals by crawling on the floor and no one worries about that. The priest and deacon sing in deep resonance—liturgies which honour the sacredness of Christ, and all is dim, candle lit even in the middle of the day. There is no question that a non-Orthodox can receive communion and inclusivity is not even attempted. But instead, dinky loaves baked with imprinted stamps are given to those outside the fold to eat on departure. In time my mother left Orthodoxy, disillusioned by the sense of a monopoly of truth she felt this denomination was increasingly building. And there was the problem of myself to consider—a daughter, ordained and empowered as a Christian leader in the Anglican Church. But in her later years she became a proficient icon writer and produced many beautiful works as she existed in a kind of fusion between the two traditions.

And then there is Roman Catholicism which I have brushed with at various points on my pilgrimage. I appreciate the more visceral yet oddly honest depictions of the crucifixion, of a Christ in an act of torture which must have been agony. I love Mary in her sky-blue robes, the humanity of the saints and the detox of the weekly confession ritual. When I started my own ordained life, being Catholic felt far more authentic to the city where I was working (Liverpool), and the churches were often more vibrant. Next door to the cold concrete barn where I was based as curate, was St Joseph the Worker's Catholic Church. There was a large sculpture of St Joey, as he was affectionately known, on the exterior of the building. A fascinating saint, St Joseph is often identified as the unofficial midwife (for who else was there to deliver the Christ child), a man of practicalities and faithfulness, who refused, after a bit of persuasion from an angel, to abandon his shamed woman.

I was quickly sought out by Fr Vin, an over-sized, sweaty and warm-hearted priest. He welcomed me into his church community. Every week I would trot next door to have a brew with the secretary in the office and many others who would drop in. Before long I was visiting all the Catholic parishioners as well as my own, some of the most resilient and kindly people I have ever met. This included Kath, a devout stalwart of the church, whose cluttered house was filled with the most wonderful religious kitsch that I had ever seen. There was not a rosary, saint statue, relic or jar of holy water that Kath hadn't purchased from her many pilgrimages and coach trips over the years. But she and many others embraced me when I arrived on their doorstep, welcomed like a long-lost cousin. I was continually pestered to go on pilgrimage to Lourdes and before I knew it was attending my first proper wake. Nervous, the only dead body I had seen prior to this, had been my father's ten years before, I went in trepidation only to realize that sitting around with a whisky and corned beef butties, an open coffin in the middle of the room, was just so normal in this place.

One of my distinctive memories was being invited to celebrate shared services and at a time where ordained young women were still something of an oddity in the Church of England, let alone in Catholic circles, it was a brave move on Vin's part. But in a city where so many are battered by life, no one seemed to mind, and I was liturgically and socially embraced. On Easter Eve I sang the long Proclamation, known as the Exsultet, during the vigil in the Roman Mass. Traditionally, this is sung by those newly ordained (which was me, so appropriate), and I carried the pillar candle into a darkened church before a whole congregation who were eagerly awaiting the joy of Christ being raised, yet again from the dead. Delighted to be asked, I was initially incapacitated by anxiety and the task in hand. Music is not my forte and I have never enjoyed singing solos in public. Luckily for me, my fiancé helped me navigate through what seemed like a musical minefield for weeks beforehand. When I was ordained as priest the following year, St Joseph's threw me a party of gargantuan magnanimity as only true Scousers can. The love shown moved me to tears and the "take home" learning being that when people radiate something of divine life it doesn't really matter what church they belong too. The radical book about being a priest given to me by the congregation and signed by Vin I still possess today.

Word leaders

I am trying to write a sermon on one of the trickiest passages in the Bible—the beginning of John's Gospel. As I ponder what "the Word made flesh" might mean for the congregation this morning, my mind returns to a novel I have just finished reading. *For Thy Great Pain Have Mercy on My Little Pain* is the story of two women who lived in fourteenth-century Norfolk. Both were mystics who experienced profoundly the love as well as the pain of knowing God. Using different kinds of communication, they tried to describe that and were misunderstood because of it. The famous anchoress Julian of Norwich wrote her visions or *shewings* after a serious illness. The other, less familiar was Margery Kempe, wife and mother of 14 children. Margery's visions of Christ's sufferings were vocally expressed only in the public square, for she could neither read nor write. Her visions alienated her from husband, family and friends partly because her chaotic and continuous crying was because she felt Jesus' sufferings so acutely. And she "preached", something inconceivable as well as dangerously heretical for a woman to do at that time. Hauled in front of the Archbishop of York and other institutional dignitaries, she spoke truth to power to her own detriment.

At 21, when my vocation was emerging, I too had a passionate calling to preach and to lead worship. I was opinionated, stubborn and resilient, and I needed to be because at that time there were plenty of people who believed women did not have a public voice in the space of the Church. Thirty years on, I try to remember the privilege of a captive congregation, people who have chosen decisively to listen to spiritual reflection, words about the depth of what it means to be alive and to hear the good news of Christ. Every time I stand at the lectern my aim is to connect *the* story of faith with the faith of *their* stories using as much creativity as I can.

Over the years, I have been moved in the core of my being by good description but also repelled by the atrophy which some words unhelpfully present. Words from childhood, thankfully no longer used a great deal now, carried the unkind weight of terrible judgment upon another—"fornication" and "slovenly" being two I remember. Now my aim is to craft beautiful and careful words alongside music and image, to create the rituals we, in my profession, call worship. It is an invitation to offer a way into grace and to exploring faith.

And are we really "miserable sinners", unworthy to scrabble around under the table to gather up the scraps of God's gifts, as the Book of Common Prayer Communion service tells us every time I bless bread and wine? And what exactly is "propitiation", a word my tongue has got itself around after years in ministry. I have wondered as I repeat these words whether these are proving a further harmful quiver of arrows to someone's already damaged soul? But as I have matured in both faith and profession an acceptance has settled, knowing that all the words we use which attempt to explain or excuse who God is will always be inadequate to describe that ultimate Mystery. But, if we catch, like a feather in the breeze, a resonance, through a metaphor or ritual, of what we know deep inside ourselves, then that language holds its power.

I have got into poetry recently. In our frantic and frenetic age, we are introduced to forms of words we need to work at, to spend time with. The American scholar and theologian Eugene Peterson describes poetry as a discipline which uses words in ways which are different from the ordinary functionality of everyday speech. Rather than convey information, poetry attempts to create communion, to create relationship, heal and restore, shape beauty and form truth. It is, he says, every priest's work. Poetry makes people stop to ponder because it uses words in ways which is often larger than the often-limited language of the everyday. Poetry looks for the pause and can lead us into new perspectives on divine life. It is the same with liturgy. The Psalms are poems, and the *Poetry Unbound* podcast, with its thoughtful, unfolding commentary, has become a current spiritual oasis. Words put together in unconventional ways slow us down as does church language when we say it collectively. Worship is one of the only forums in the world where people undertake both an individual as well as a shared reflective journey because of them.

But what clergy do is help their congregation to make sense of their own stories, and if those are painful, then those communal words help absorb these as they become experiences shared and set in context with the memory of others.

And this happens through the multitude of other elements which make up what we describe as "worship", choirs and bells and rituals. Over the years, as leader and participant, worship in its various forms has left me both numb in its blandness as well as moving me to tears, catalysing a complete emotional journey just as a good film might do. We leave church with our "issues" chiselled out somehow, yet also strangely repaired and we are given hope for the rest of the day. Clergy craft scenarios through ritual, and hope God is felt to connect with those who have come. Last Sunday the chance of anointing with blessed oil and prayers for wholeness and healing (in its widest form), I felt something greater surround me, far more than my own clumsy efforts. I had dispensed with the set words and created my own, calling people by name. Something happened and I know the 19 others who were there felt it too.

Rituals like this work the earth of the heart. Doing things slowly reminds me of the measured pace of monastic life. There is a stepping down, away from a life of rush. In these places, words, worship, rituals are slow as time is taken over them. One Franciscan monastery at which I recently spent some time used so much incense its fragrance sat like a misty apparition on the air itself, soaking into the clothes of those of us who sat in the cold chapel. It helped me into a different state of mind and heart.

The language of worship uses metaphor, which reveres ambiguity and remains an antidote against certainty. We have grown fearful of our imagination when it comes to faith, so many insisting on black and white, and this is why I love poetry so much because the sense of the sacred feels very much alive in so much of it. People on the edge of religious institutions also need to participate in rituals where they can transcend themselves through the hearing of the sacred through the fusion of the ordinary. Sensitive priests are tuned into producing occasions as possibilities which open rather than shut down a variety of "spirituality". Here are a few from my own recent ministry.

It is Maundy Thursday, always a poignant and extended service which leads into the drama of Good Friday, set up as the light dims. The tender washing of feet is something clergy do for those in their congregations, and two years ago I led that service with a colleague. We had our own feet washed and washed those of others, and somewhere along the road we realized we had not factored in time to put our socks and shoes back on. So, we left them off and led the rest of the service in feet cold and bare against the stone floor. There was something organic and reverent about this, marking an occasion of remembered significance. Another time at our local primary school in Spirituality Week, each class had been tasked to think up an interactive prayer station. These had been set up in the school hall and members of the community invited in. "Would you like to come into my tent?" a five-year-old asked me, holding out her hand. I stooped down and entered the flimsy plastic play space. With a sweep of her hand, she showed me an array of cuddly animals, sharks and snakes and flamingos. "This is where I bless the animals," she said. "Would you like to help me?" I could have wept at the generous invitation into a ritual by this tiny person who had so naturally and without hesitation put herself in the place of priest, no holds barred. Poets, priests and children know, as Jesus did when a frowned-upon woman poured expensive oil on his feet, that symbolic acts undertaken reverently, matter.

Parish clergy, through worship have an extraordinary opportunity to provide these spaces along with others, for people to meet the divine life within as well as outside of themselves. I believe in doing this as imaginatively as possible however we do that—we owe this to our people who turn up faithfully, often burned out from their week's work and thirsty to be nourished rather than bored with irrelevance or churchiness. Good worship often takes a strange courage—the stepping out to experiment with something different. One Sunday I set up seven bowls of water. Alongside them were words which symbolized the "things in the way" which prevent us from flourishing into the people we believe we are trying to become with the help of a strength outside of ourselves. The invitation was to dip hands into each bowl and to reflect on seven words placed alongside each one, words which described something of the ruts we fall into, often inadvertently—guilt, anger, despair, grudges, shame.

Many of us love and need to be occasionally taken to the moon and back with soaring cathedral choirs singing St Matthew's Passion, but often the best "worship" has been in the humble and tiny rituals described above. Julian of Norwich was no exception either; her hazelnut metaphor is perhaps overly used, but that is so because it speaks of a tiny ordinary thing which holds a strange truth. Through the revelations of Julian and the rantings of Margery, we experience God. This extract from the book is a beautiful example of how God can be discovered in words made flesh:

> I remembered being a wife and mother, rinsing the herring for dinner, using a sharp knife to scrape away the scales before hanging the fish above the fire. Days later I'd find scales between the stone flags of the floor, stuck to the wall, caught in my woollen shawl. Now, when I remembered how they were everywhere, I saw that it was just the same with God's love. God is not a being on high, to whom we must raise our eyes, God is everywhere, in all things, including us. We are clad in the goodness of God, so closely that our souls and God are one thing, and that this one-ing is the most important thing to understand. For we are oned with God, we can never be divided from him.*

---

* Victoria Mackenzie, *For Thy Great Pain Have Mercy on My Little Pain* (London: Bloomsbury, 2023), p. 108.

1 3

Epiphany

January is a beautifully black month. The trees show their dark skeletons, stark against a watery sky. Now, I get up early to run my four miles, through parks where the gentle branches of fir trees reach out, gently cheering me on through the gloom. I jog past, nodding to early morning walkers with their dogs in illuminated collars, throbbing in neon blues and yellows, canine spectres chasing circles with one another on this winter's morning. A still month is January, as though the world, tired after the past year, is wanting rest, the earth giving up its perpetual cycle of growth, gone to ground like a ship sunken beneath the surface.

Twenty-three years ago, my daughter was born—on 6 January—the Feast of the Epiphany. The due date had been Christmas Day—a day others thought strangely appropriate for the child of two members of clergy. But mysteriously happy in the primordial wetness of the womb she remained for longer than she should perhaps, and that is an extraordinary fact for one who now dislikes being alone. As mothers do, I remember that night. Born at one a.m., the later hours of that evening were spent doubled up in pain, as I had been on the maternity ward too long, in a confused non-understanding that I should have sought help earlier but did not. Apparently, my threshold for pain is high. Within minutes of expressing an agony I could no longer bear, I was taken down to the depths of that hospital, my husband flustered and desperate, trying to find an entrance as main doors were locked at that time in the night.

Like food can be, birth is a leveller. Wherever our origins might lie as women, whatever our careers or accents are, at the point of birth bodies go through the same natural rhythms of automatic contraction, breath and push. However composed we are on ordinary days, here is the moment when we are at our most vulnerable in every sense, makeup-less, sweaty, primal fluid and bodily entrances displayed for strangers and lovers to see. For moments, maybe hours, we lose ourselves, groaning like whales, as others ease the passage of another's life in a quiet reassurance that all is well, even when it is not. Midwives have been here a thousand times before. And before the day dawned the miraculous fleshy beauty of a baby, wrinkled and red, was placed into my arms.

The end of things often allows the beginning of something else and each of life's stages heralds another. Now my daughter is a vibrant young woman. She is blond and petite, hilarious and balanced. She works hard, plays hard, is mischievous and already intuitive. Passionate about her chosen profession creates a link with my father's side of the family—she is a trainee solicitor with a good law degree behind her. She was my epiphany too, my firstborn, bringing me constant illumination on the world through the learning of motherhood and now as a companion on the way.

On 6 January, the Church celebrates the Feast of the Epiphany—a day described as a "major festival". Indeed that comforting meal of tea and toast after the birth could not have tasted more delicious. Faith or not, everyone loves the story of the Wise Men, Kings, Magi whatever you want to call them. Men probably of Zoroastrian faith they studied the Jewish scriptures as well as the stars. For some bizarre reason, they felt the urge to set out on a perilous and long journey to bring gifts for a child they did not know. These three are depicted on many a Christmas card, popular culture loving their exotic and unusual enigma. Scholarship cannot tell whether they knew one another prior to the trip. Their gifts symbolized an alternative kingship for Christ (gold), frankincense (holiness) and myrrh (suffering and healing). And for Eve, an appropriate day to be born for I like to think of this in an alternative way regarding her future profession—that she will earn a good living as a lawyer (gold), bring healing to many weighed down by legal anxiety (myrrh), and within all of that there will be a unique contribution to the world (frankincense).

At the point of birth, a sacred silence descends upon the scene once the writhing and chaos ceases. It is both intimate and understood, emotional but overwhelmingly physical too. And all a spiritual experience whatever someone believes. So often relief that the risky journey is over, like those Wise Men who fell to their knees in gratitude as they reached the stable.

It is an amazing and profound thing to ease new human life into this world, or even to witness it, and those who have done it rarely forget the moment which can only ever be their own.

But what happens when birth goes wrong? I remember conducting the funeral of a baby. Standing on the doorstep, praying for the mysterious strength to be found to say the right words. Or else to sit in a silence of offered solidarity when words fail because of the reality of pain, because of the secret guilt for my own healthy child, because of the deficiency of religious sentiments and a danger of badly chosen platitudes. The Church does not always have a language for the variations of our humanness, or the nuances of our emotional lives, save in the gritty rawness of the Psalms. Our priestly help is often simple, if not easy, the sincerity of good listening and the shaping of ritual which may help move the process of grief on in dignity and hope. On a damp winter day, I led in the small pink coffin and described the beautiful metaphor of the cherry tree which shares its delicate blossoms for such a short time each year. And in that natural beauty, a brevity is immortalized, a collective memory created. Most residents were awed by the fragile beauty of the pink trees which lined the road where I used to live. But that day they could not go there. It was about staying in the deadness of what felt a harsh, brutal courage of allowing the simple kindness of others' efforts to carry and soothe in a blessing only they could own. It is the tenderness of others which sits unnoticed behind so many things.

My daughter's name was Eve; it means life. On her birthday, we went to one of Grayson Perry's exhibitions—art inspired by different themes from ordinary life. Perry thought up the idea of an online art club, encouraging members of the public (with a few celebrities thrown in), to submit works of art to ease mental anxiety and other struggles during lockdown. Much was brought to birth, as creative urges and buried talents were, like forgotten heirlooms in an attic, brought into the light through Perry's own gifts of inclusivity and affirmation. Like the gifts of the Wise Men, the experience of reading and viewing some of the works felt rich, holy and healing all at once. That day I was feeling tired and weighed down after two bad nights' sleep, awake with worry about a colleague leaving me and a leaking roof of the property where my mother lived. But this art, in all its defiant resilience, pulled me out of my depression and brought me hope through its creativity and humanity. Art has the capacity to stretch our minds and our sense of being alive. The exhibition did both of those things for us, leaving us in tears at several of the works. A drawing describing the relentlessness of graduate job applications with the hardness of the constant rejection, a sculpture made by a father-and-son team, the latter later taking his own life, and a gigantic, knitted sculpture of Sandringham elevated that understanding that many have of the craft as a grannyfied and frumpy activity.

Every day we bring things to birth, we need to create beginnings and to end and engineer things which need to cease, relationships, projects and even ways of life which should have reached the finishing line years ago. But often we cannot bear to do that, refusing to allow things or people to slip away, out of sight, out of our lives, as even difficult things hold the comfort of company or familiarity. Even though these may bring us strife, worry or wear us down, their significance in our life's eroded beauty is too great to dispense with.

Blessing is part and parcel of a priest's specific role and often comes at the end of a liturgy, as a completion, a strengthening to be set on our way again. When I anoint people with oil blessed for the specific purpose to heal and to help, it is as if I am caressing fragments of pain or yearning that others bring but cannot put into words. A humble bishop did that for a group of us once, in his rose-scented garden; intimate, the gentle touch somehow held the whole of me and had me in tears.

1 4

Ritual

My maternal grandparents were precious people to me, now residents solely in my memories. I stayed with them often during my young life. Like many people do, as they grew reluctantly as well as peacefully towards old age, they had a daily routine. That kept them going, enabling them to feel happy in the elegiac calm of every day. Each morning my grandfather would plod upstairs to the book-lined bedroom I slept in to deliver morning tea. The tea arrived on a tray in an exquisite china set with tiny milk jug and sugar bowl, even though I have never taken sugar in tea in my life. Then he would plod downstairs again, to deliver tea to my grandmother and sit in his bedroom chair where they would read a section from some kind of meditative writing. A few careful verses were enough spirituality to chew on through their gentle days, and in the winter the open fire would be lit—a slight oddity in a bedroom perhaps— as well as the fact that the fire only burnt for as long as my grandmother had her breakfast in bed. But I loved this morning ritual, appreciating being included in the safest of spaces. It felt almost sacred.

What is it that changes a routine into a ritual? Routines are ways of behaviour that we construct, often with the good practice in building an ordered and healthy life. Putting a child to bed, with bath, story, maybe prayers, to promote good rest and calm at the end of a day, is one. But this is not necessarily ritual. Rituals invite us to see further significance in their attempt to communicate an important message through symbols, specific words and actions, many around rites of passage. Ritual provides us with the space, through regulated and methodical actions which, often boundaried, allow us to explore that which cannot be contained—our emotions, spirituality and belief systems. Rituals help us to slow down and to see that which we fail to see, often because our lives these days are raced through at such a pace. All of us participate in ritual whether we are people who have a faith or not and whether these are regular or occasional. Often ritual uses metaphors, allowing our imaginations to work through poetry which connects us with the deepest of stories which speak of the truth of existence.

Personal or collective, these feel precious occasions, whose rules must be adhered to but never oppressively. We often hear someone say "It's an annual ritual", meaning an occasion we ourselves understand, an experience which, if it does not happen, our souls mourn. Visiting National Trust properties with my oldest friend whenever we meet becomes less of a middle-class pastime but more the remembrance of the time when, as teenagers we grasped a sense of the world being beautiful and ourselves on the edge of something as we lazed around their sumptuous green spaces in hot sunshine. Tea and cake form part of the ritual, as food so often belongs here too.

Faith-based communities love ritual and in church we often overly worry about whether what we are offering is understood by people new to its culture. But certainty has always been the enemy of ritual as well as, strangely, faith. Maria Balshaw, Director of the Tate Foundation, expresses similar thoughts surrounding contemporary art. Trust others' curiosity and intelligence, she says. If we explain everything, we are in danger of stripping away the complexities within the life that we live, we rob and drain the mystery from the art or the ritual. We send out messages too—that certain things are not worth working at or working for—creativity, faith, truth, language. Enigma and signs are part of life and learning to read them is part of being human. Ritual helps us to see the truth of a situation and to plant seeds of significance. Trust its autonomy and power to call to attention a moment that needs to be marked or threshold crossed for it to feel safe or to be remembered. Baptism as well as the last rites before death are two examples.

Driving across town, summoned by four desperate siblings and three grandchildren who have managed to make it to be with their mother and grandmother who is dying, my heart is racing. I send up a quick prayer for the traffic to be unclogged, for there to be a parking space at the vast hospital where she is. I run in, mask on (it is still Covid time), and my collar acts as "open sesame" as I find my way past the security guards and into the room several floors up. I open my book and begin to speak the words that priests understand as "final prayers"—that someone's soul might be at peace, might allow itself to travel over the threshold between life and into what is unknown. My presence somehow stops the flailing and fuss, and a silence descends. I have a tiny vial of oil, blessed and I use this now to sign the cross on Audrey who no longer looks like the person I have known. At moments like this it matters not what people believe—I am so grateful I have made it here and for what is happening to somehow be recognized as holding importance. Permission now to depart is felt, however long this might take. And then I step back, in a changed atmosphere, the time is theirs again and my job is done. Fifteen minutes of ritual unashamed and unvarnished but beautiful. I will meet them all again at the funeral.

Another time, a family feel there is a strange atmosphere in their old cottage. They are professional, intelligent and people of faith, and I have no reason to doubt their mental stability. It is not a good thing to feel uncomfortable in your own home. I offer to come and bless the house which is what they want. I find a liturgy for a house blessing, one which honours each room and its function. Whatever I do or do not believe is happening, what matters is their peace of mind. After tea and general chat, I suggest we begin. I have brought holy water, pre-blessed, and in each room, I sprinkle it, everywhere. It works, like sacred rain, water which takes on new significance, its tiny drops absorbing potential evil essences. A week later Lucia tells me everyone feels better and thanks me with a bunch of unnecessary flowers. And she tells me that someone years ago died at the foot of the stairs.

I remember as a child the rituals associated with the church year. Lighting of the Advent candles each week. Participating as the angel with blue glittery wings in the Nativity Play. Carols. The distinctive services of Holy Week with their universal themes of life—betrayal, pain, the importance of friends, the weaknesses of an institution, death, bereavement and then new life. The rituals surrounding those few days are often extraordinarily creative, and it's good to participate in them from start to finish, for the whole big story is diminished if we only listen to half of it. And then lesser festivals which remain still important in the public consciousness. Shrove Tuesday, where we no longer fast for weeks before Easter but still stuff ourselves with carb-laden pancakes. Easter Day, where we may or may not have done the Holy Week journey but still dine on lamb, visit farms with new chicks and rabbits, relish the freshness of the lime green leaves and enjoy the sharp breeze of spring. Remembrance Sunday, as everyone understands the idea of remembering and honouring those brave enough to fight in wars even if we might not agree with how it is done. Harvest because everyone gets the idea of saying thank you for food, even if we are unsure who it is we are thanking. Good ritual, like a good film script, happens when things can be said from a different place of truth and buried spaces reawaken within us.

Often those of us who are part of a religious organization are not very imaginative in terms of creating new rituals for others. And sometimes we are constrained by the rules. That alone feels like a lost opportunity especially when people come to us with the courage to ask as well as the sensitivity to recognize that in their lives there feels an occasion to mark, to hold, to share. Grayson Perry also produced *Rites of Passage*, which fused new rituals with his art. Taking place in ordinary spaces and places, it broadened an understanding of what is expected and allowed. A funeral gathering for one man before he had actually died, as friends and family gathered to tell him what he had meant to them through carefully chosen words or symbols which were posted into one of the large pots Perry has become famous for. Another episode involved teenagers making a film about how they felt about emerging into an adult world in a coming-of-age ceremony. Another took place in a sunny field as a divorcing couple, about to go their separate ways, cut a diaphanous piece of material that the artist had created; each of them kept one side of the cloth. But it symbolized the split, the end of a relationship, sensitively and poignantly with no glossing over the pain of what remains a hard and scarring experience for many.

There is a yearning within me as religious practitioner of what has been understood as traditional ritual, to develop such imaginative occasions. The regulated faith of the institution is not always very honest or open to processing pain or lament through the rituals they offer, at least in the West. For emotion is dumbed down, somewhere on the road from childhood to adulthood and we find ways of not expressing the more uncomfortable parts of being human—anger, loss, hurt being three of them. Traditional funerals aside, there are so many experiences which happen to us as human people that cry out for a closure which is healing and supportive. We need to be braver and far more imaginative. It has led several priests I know to leave the Church to offer something far freer and more expansive as they become not Church of England clergy but civil celebrants, their pastoral skills highly transferable.

But good ritual remains too—both within traditional religious institutions as well as outside of them. It provides us with tools to take out of our life a coping kit which we often strangely rediscover when life feels traumatic. My daughter, in her second year of university, described movingly going round the eight-bedroomed flat where she lived, cleansing and blessing each room after one of its residents had been taken to hospital after suddenly collapsing. That student had been judged inappropriately as a student drunk, irresponsibly taking up NHS resources at the height of the Covid pandemic. It was far from the case and remained a mystery as to why this had happened to him. Several friends felt a bad atmosphere resided in the flat for that close-knit group. At a point in her life when she has been ambivalent towards believing anything, something in the recesses of her psyche suggested the idea of a house blessing, which herself and friends officiated at themselves.

1 5

Bread

Euston was its usual travel chaos. A forecourt packed with those going to and from. A glance at the overhead departure boards became a realization that something was afoot with train after train being cancelled. Failure on the line at Watford Gap. Running from one platform to another I found a seat, sweating with relief, and sat down. Reserved seating had disappeared and surrounding me were a group of lads. Animated, with a sense of release from their ordinary lives, they were going to watch the cricket in Manchester. They were all from an extended Asian family, and we got chatting, partly out of relief to have boarded a train that might just move. One man had a small business, another was a tube driver on the Central Line, and one had worked in high-end hotels throughout the world. Two were particularly lively and soon beer and samosas appeared, generously offered round, the laughter and chat increasing in volume as they told me how they were all related to one another—brothers, nephews, friends and how this trip happened most years. Round us were others, quiet witnesses to our cheerful sharing. A shy Pentecostal pastor, squashed like a sardine in the middle of this delight, and an older couple, bemused in tolerant good humour what they had found themselves amongst. I refused to tell the lads my profession, teasing them with details of drinking wine and dressing up, telling them I was a vicar just minutes before I arose to leave. There was magic in this spontaneous and unexpected sharing, and that mysterious dynamic which happens when Brits are thrown together in a bit of adversity—they start to talk as community is created.

We walk into others' communions all the time. When priests celebrate the sacrament, they use words which ask others to come and share, inviting a step towards some kind of intimacy, a drawing near with whatever faith they possess. I am always looking for connections and, on that afternoon, I became the one who was invited instead, a guest, as were the others, seated around the train table which became our altar, a natural eucharistic feast. Two priests (myself and the pastor) were present, yet neither of us was the president. Priests are called to see the holiness in these moments, to highlight and to herald them, whether they are in the camp or outside of it. Communion on that Euston afternoon was outside of the camp because it didn't happen in church.

When Christians eat bread and drink wine, they participate symbolically in Christ's life, death and resurrection. They do this repeatedly, week after week and sometimes day after day. We recite the words "living sacrament" in the prayer which proceeds the partaking. Bread is a universal language around the world, French, pitta, naan, trendy sour dough. I painted a picture a few years back which still hangs on my kitchen wall. It is a pictorial version of the great feast Christ celebrated in a field, the story of the Feeding of the 5,000, blessing and distributing a very small amount of food which miraculously feeds a whole crowd. In my picture, the number 5,000 is created by two mackerel (which wrap themselves around the figure five) and five loaves of distinct kinds (which become the noughts). Sharing bread and wine in church is only understood when it is a real dynamic that we do to keep us and others physically and spiritually alive. It is only understood when we connect it to the events of life and death which we live through too. Bread is the product of sun and the salty sweat of the hands that knead it.

So many people I know now regularly bake bread. There is something, it seems, about the essential nature of it that resonates with most of us. It is a global food, and in its simplicity and complexity humanity has the capacity to reformulate the phenomenon that is bread almost anywhere, ingredients distinctive as well as dependant on culture and climate. In Egypt and Morocco it is normal to deposit your dough in a communal oven, the baker collecting it later, on the way home from shopping or work. In West Africa it was initially intriguing for me to eat French sticks as the main bread staple, this originating from the time of colonization.

Bread, like love, cannot be rushed; it has its own inner life. It rises mysteriously only to be pummelled down by kneading hands who mould and shape it into what it needs to be. Good love does that too, if only we let it, life pulls and punches but then we are loved back into some kind of shape by parents, partners and friends. There is a profound spiritual lesson within a mixing bowl. It reminds me that eating is a universal experience every human person must do to stay alive. There is a strange paradox going on with good bread—it is so precious, yet so dispensable as we throw out stale crusts for the birds who are blessed by God in the Bible too. I have friends who always bring to my home a baked loaf, along with a bottle of good Rioja—a beautiful offering of everyday grace.

Bread, then, is not so much what we offer but how we approach the offering. Sister Rosemary, a joyful bundle of overweight love, holds a fondness for me. Once a month, my parents and I would go to the convent where she was the cook for Sunday lunch—an abundant affair of soup, roast meat and traditional British puddings. My father taught his students how to be vicars there on residential weekends. This ebullient nun swept my eight-year-old self up in her ample habited bosom, stained with blackcurrants and flour, and allowed me into the vast convent kitchen, an enviable National-Trust style affair with huge Belfast sinks, wooden table in the middle and tins of freshly baked pies. We ate, and I, the only child, surrounded by men in cords and my mother, masked my shyness as doughy rolls were broken open, steam exploding from the middle of them, the perfect food for a chilly autumn afternoon. But it was not so much the food that drew me but the expansive and maternal warmth of Sister Rosemary. I can picture her face now, round and sweaty, anxious to make sure the young men were pleased with the stodgy lunches she produced and perhaps her seeing me satisfied some hidden desire for supressed motherhood. Convents hold distinctive smells and that homely room where we ate, with its scrubbed, plain tables, worn ironware held always aromas of steamed jam sponge, cabbage and carbolic soap.

There is nothing more comforting or uplifting than the smell of baking bread. Making is elemental, kneading is therapeutic. We can pound our anger, create plaited patterns and insert raisins or herbs, having fun with the kids. Bread reminds me that there is a spirituality at the very core of ordinary things, and this is why the Bible brims with such images, of water turning to wine and God's people stuffing flatbreads hastily into bags before escaping from slavery. Bread provides a metaphor for life that is both simple as well as mysteriously complex. Biblically it is the elements used in bread making which have provided brilliant teaching aids for centuries, wheat, yeast and salt. Oil is a symbol of the good life, understood as a blessing and abundant gift in the same way wine, figs and honey are. Paul Hollywood, in his cookbook *Bread*, says, "The most successful dinner party I've ever had was after I had baked a batch of sourdough baguettes at work one morning. I brought them home, put them on the table that evening, opened some red wine and served apples, cheese, wine and pate. Everyone left saying it was the most enjoyable meal they'd ever had."* Something happens when good bread comes out onto the table which soothes and makes life feel sweet. It makes us feel better and less ravished by life even for a few hours. It provides a talking point and often a place of connection.

It remains an obscenity to deny people their daily bread, just as it remains an abuse to deny people the reminder of the presence of Jesus in their lives. One day, in a conservative church in South Africa, I discovered a member of the congregation had been barred from communion because they were going through a divorce. Even now there are members of my own congregation who choose not to hold out their hands and I do not wish to pry. But they come for a blessing at least, that is a form of hunger associated with bread, a longing from someone for inclusion and spiritual closeness which resides way down deep.

Sharing bread and wine forms the basis of many a church ritual. But how we share it often feels overly managed, with the culture of church insisting we spend too much time with our clanking silver vessels and anaemic wafers. But mostly the receiving of that tiny piece of meaning retains its importance for each who receives it as they hold out their hands. As priest, I hover, awaiting what is needed for each. I like to use names when I can, or if I can't remember, to ask, so bread is equated with individuality as well as universality. Some cannot bear the intimacy of that moment. They look up, or down as the moment becomes too bright, like a mistaken glance at the sun, whilst many, perhaps because I know their stories, meet my gaze as soul and food connect.

---

* Paul Hollywood, *Bread* (London: Bloomsbury, 2013), p. 6.

1 6

Furious feast and the failure of fast

There is nothing like a pancake when one is especially hungry. From my childhood I remember that steaming, starchy loveliness we ate with crunchy sugar and sharp lemons on the Tuesday which precedes Lent, the season of cleansing, guilt and failed discipline. Pancake Day is the popular name for its more religious sister, Shrove Tuesday, the day the faithful would peer into their cupboards to use up all the rich food accumulated before the six-week fast before Easter, when luxuries like meat, dairy products, sugar and any alcohol would not be consumed. Eating less and praying more was the aim of the game. I love Shrove Tuesday and have celebrated many different variations of this, pancake races on a playground in a village school, pancakes in a men's refuge, and more recently the frenzy of frying these for a hundred people amidst activities in a crammed and steamy church hall. This latter was followed by some restored balm of 30 minutes calm in a quieter church as explanation of this feast was communicated. A short but powerful (strange to the uninitiated) ritual of ash on foreheads (a day early) was enacted as parents and kids were invited to grasp that moment of gravitas when we are challenged to ponder our own transitory lives on Ash Wednesday—the beginning of Lent.

Food in my own clergy childhood was traditional but plentiful, usually homemade and with fresh fruit and vegetables from our enormous garden. My mother's solace had always been growing her own and in an era before the trendy irony of "the artisan", a description of high-quality goods which often only the middle classes can afford, I enjoyed hearty food from what have become rare gems—the local butcher's shop and produce grown and baked by non-working women involved in the Women's Institute.

Growing up through the 1970s and '80s a typical day's food for me would include some kind of cooked breakfast, even fishfingers (my mother believed in a good start), something I found a deep trial as I often felt so nervous for school, my cramping stomach muscles just could not cope. A cooked school lunch, toast and something sweet on return and then "supper" (a key difference in how the evening meal is described by working and middle-class kids). Supper consisted of a classic British dish, such as beef stew, and there was always dessert—usually stewed fruit and milk pudding. The expansiveness of global food choice, the supermarket and the idea that every person might become a household chef were all unusual in the Cornish town where I grew up. Wine, cream cakes, chocolate and crisps were all considered treats, although my family often dined out well with other clergy colleagues on Sundays, and every now and then we would venture to a local hotel—the Brookdale. There groaning heart-attack type desserts would be served on a creaking silver trolley and I felt heaven had truly arrived. However bad a day becomes, if there is food, or the promise of it, in a fridge or cupboard I consider myself blessed.

It is impossible to live a good clergy life without being prepared to eat. In this life there is not much room for abstinence as we constantly anticipate social events where food is at the centre, parish lunches, celebratory afternoon teas, harvest suppers, and in more recent years, quizzes which are completed with fish and chip dinners, curry nights, cheese and wine; the list goes on.

In church circles the belief that food is gift always is deeply embedded. But that does not always represent the reality of food anxiety and unfair distribution. Harvest is a bitter-sweet festival where we thank the divine for the earth's abundance while collecting for the food bank. Food becomes anxiety for those who go without so their kids can eat, and resentment comes when every choice must be the cheapest. Others find food stressful. My daughter's eighteen-year-old friend who struggles with anorexia, her mother desperate with sadness in the wasteful tragedy of it all. And it was not gift for me as I became bulimic at 18, a condition which stalked me through my twenties, delivering the message that my body was always to feel less than satisfactory. It was not until a revelatory moment when it dawned on me from within my own shadowland that this condition was a processing of a buried grief and things got better.

Social events surrounding food are the beating heart of any ecclesiastical community and they often unobtrusively offer other things, a gathering place where the lonely can park their solitude for a little while, the invitation to be a part of some indecipherable mystery or just a little kindness. Poor churches often have little else to give and communicate an unarticulated sense of mission through this offering outwards. I have delighted in every congregation among which I have been priest and the food they offer, from coconut chicken to hog roasts. All is a delight and becomes a strange kind of learning about different food cultures, hurt and hardship but all served through a natural kindness.

Being a priest has provided the opportunity and safe passage to sit down with many different people over food. The harvest supper in a rural village, our tiny son sleeping in a basket as we tucked into chicken stew from someone's farm and local cider; when overheated, we escaped outside to the starlit night and the sounds of hooting owls in the trees above. Burns Night, of all places in the bowels of a concrete inner city church, as almost one hundred people were fed haggis and neeps and whisky. And even Prosecco in a cathedral, the visionary dean realizing that money had to be made by hiring out the cavernous building for corporate events. This year I will share at another church in the Iftar—the traditional meal eaten during Ramadan—where Muslims break their fast from food and drink after sunset, an event which invites people of all faiths and none to a traditional feast of dates, curry and other delights.

Feast is a concept which seeks to celebrate human life, united in the fact that every human being needs to eat to get through, and that if we can do this well then life can feel less relentless. Surprise encounters sometimes abound over food as a friend of mine bought a random stranger his lunch in a café as part of her own "50 at 50" list. The man delighted, struck up conversation and a beautiful moment was created in those two lives that day.

Theories of fasting have now taken over the secular world, hopefully in healthy ways, through the promotion of sensible periods of food abstinence considered beneficial for body and mind, even though the spiritual is not often connected with its practice. In my priestly life, I have given up things for Lent, fasted for whole days at a time to raise money for charity or, dressed up in sanctimony, simply for the purpose of losing weight. I like the feeling of being in control and of the appreciation of taste and food when eating resumes. Fasting is one such phenomenon which, on its healthy side, suggests we might need to rest our bodies from their appetites and to regain control of something which has run away from us, like a puppy we find difficult to train. For me fasting is a daily discipline I must be patient with, but without it, I cannot embrace the sense of feast with much integrity. Food remains a dark love for so many of us. It is often all that is left to enjoy at the end of a day and at the end of a life.

In the Bible there is both feast and fast. The idea that food can powerfully move beyond categories of rich and poor. Poor people feed others in the Bible (the widow who feeds Elijah), copious amounts are produced by not very much (Feeding of the 5,000), and even in desperate vulnerability there is something to eat (manna in the wilderness). Food is a ritual at the heart of our worship, even if we have lost the earthy vitality of it in a sip of wine and tiny wafer. These days for me it is not really about what we eat but how we do it. Eating alone can be heartbreaking for those who yearn to share the feast. Eating together can also be a trial and is not necessarily an indication of a mutual togetherness—just think about the Last Supper. But food also provides an invitation to participate in the building up of morale, of hope and is about the creation of community, whether familiar or formulating.

It is the end of December and the Christmas tree has that dehydrated look, its branches sagging slightly like a tired waitress at the end of her shift. The room has seen a party or two at the end of last year, welcoming the choir as a thank you for all their dulcet tones throughout the year, dinner for a couple who just needed an evening away from caring for their elderly parents. The weather app says that New Year's Day is set to be grey drizzle. But this matters not, for every year my family head to the edge of Manchester, where the city meets the wilds of the Peak District. We meet with a group of longstanding friends, enjoy a bracing, cobweb-sweeping walk (whatever the weather), stop off at the pub for a hot toddy, then pile back for a huge meal. Our friend Pat, a northern girl, is Queen of Pies—no one makes pastry like her. We return to sip tea, drink wine, eat cheese-and-onion pies, beef stew and trifle. This annual ritual feels a generous, heartening way to begin any year. Surrounded by the warmth and nonjudgment of people kind to the core, it has long felt more eucharistic than many a dry church service of Holy Communion. And each time, as the day ends, I feel the sharp keenness of this feast and an opportunity to meet the unfolding year, whatever that might bring.

1 7

Chinese lanterns

A friend gave me a postcard of Chinese lanterns, seed pods, each one a different colour and in a progressive state of decay. The last lantern's papery shell is almost gone, and displaying the delicacy of a butterfly's wing, reveals the seed inside. A seed which appears solid and still strong. That image seems to be a symbol of many older people I know. Those of the older generation who understand their own mortality, often as illness and physical decline feel harder to shake off. So many older people I know are like these seed pearls—a little wrinkled but wise, resilient and full of humour with a healthy perspective on themselves and the world.

Churches are full of older and sometimes very old people. New retirees often run the church these days, still in good health and with some vigour, they carry forward their professional expertise as well as their human experience. If they arrive (and remain), you are fortunate indeed. Then there are older people who cannot stop being "the professional", unable to put that down to allow others to step in, a new and dangerous self-identity. And if their professional lives have been unhappy or dissatisfying, they seem to work this out, patronizing others and swinging apparent power around. It can make clergy life difficult. But our charge too, is to respect all, to listen to all, to be patient with all and harder still, to love all. I try to do this but sometimes just run out of emotional energy dealing with everyone's complexes and soapbox issues. But mostly I deal with this in the knowledge that all of us are double-edged swords, holding blunt as well as sharp sides and holding talents as well as damage.

Today though I am visiting Betty whose ninety-ninth birthday is in a few weeks. Betty is well known in our church and much loved. She is mentally astute but walks with the use of a frame now. She is a regular participant in groups we hold to encourage older people to reflect on a variety of subject matter and she rarely misses a Sunday. Betty has been a teacher, is now a widow, and always has some interesting memory to share. This year we are journeying through Lent looking at the spiritual significance of everyday objects. Clergy often do not have time to regularly visit as George Herbert would have done on his horse each afternoon, and if they do, it is only when someone is in genuine crisis or at death's door. But I like to diary time for it for there is often a mysterious abundance within an older life. There can be a contemplation, a life lived more slowly which slows me down too. I feel a dignity, a measuredness associated with the inevitable simplification of having to give things up or put things down. Living life like this can mean more time to recognize the simple blessings a life can hold.

For me it feels important always to carry a sense of natural affirmation. Kathleen Norris mentions in *The Cloister Walk*, for example, that older people are not often told they are beautiful. This slips away from our vocabulary as we grow up. We are wired in to tell every baby they are beautiful even if they are not; we recognize beauty in slim nymphs who wear clothes that look gorgeous because of it, but we do not often find the courage to tell an older, larger, scarred or disabled person they too, are beautiful. Somehow, we find that embarrassing or insincere. And that is why the ministry of those who work in care homes, hospitals and as hairdressers and nail technicians are of so much value because they work with the tangible results of making those who are physically fragile and old feel better about themselves.

I love visiting because more than anything it is about listening to the stories of others. Often, someone reveals just a little of that story and I respond by telling just a little of mine. Sometimes vulnerability opens like a floodgate (on both sides) and the judging of how appropriate this is on any given occasion needs to be judged in the now. But I have rarely regretted baring my soul, for despite the increasing professionalism of the clergy, which generates an "us and them" situation, I believe our own undefendedness and scars can provide a pathway towards hope for others. For me this is about searching always for connection, for when connection happens relationship is built, and friendship becomes a possibility. "We are", as Padraig O'Tuama so beautifully puts it, "the stories we tell about ourselves, and we are more than the stories we tell about ourselves."* And we are all really, a collection of stories which overlap.

A few years ago when I was in a dry and micromanaged job outside of ordinary church life, I sought to retain my priestly heart by being a volunteer visitor for a local pastoral scheme which supported people lonely or in crisis just for a short time. Within the first service of ordination—the Ordination of Deacons—lies an exquisite phrase. It says that deacons should be "reaching into the forgotten corners of the world, that the love of God may be made visible". Doing this is to identify those people and places which remain ignored, forgotten, shelved or given up upon and to go out towards them. It is a command to go to the people and places on the edges.

Martine lived in one of these forgotten corners, an ordinary ground floor flat with the number 13 stickered on the outside. The surrounding area was scruffy—there were cars, bins, some rubbish, a cat sunning itself—an area not smart and a bit nondescript. Here was the home of the young woman I began to visit. Martine had many vulnerabilities. Rarely out of bed because of a mysterious debilitating condition which doctors could not get to the bottom of, for most of her life she had been unable to walk. With no contact with her parents or most of her family and with a history of mental illness and self-harm, she relied on carers coming in twice a day to feed, wash and clean for her. I was matched with her because Martine was creative and had expressed an interest in doing some art and craft with someone who might also have a similar background. Martine's small dog and a few good neighbours and friends provided her with additional comfort.

For various reasons I had to stop visiting Martine, a sadness to me at the time. Yet it was here in her home, a place which felt on the margins, that a surprising encounter between two very different people happened. In a society where it seems so easy to remain in our own personal spheres of reference, I got as much out of my visits to her as I hope she did. Martine was very different from me. I've had a stable upbringing. I enjoy the privilege of a body that works, my own family provides love

---

* Padraig O'Tuama, *In the Shelter: Finding a Home in the World* (London: Hodder & Stoughton, 2015), p. 230.

and support, and my working life has given me an established identity. Nevertheless, we discovered considerable connections. We both grew up in Cornwall and both of us studied art. But more than this, similar interests were described—she, like me, enjoyed cooking shows and was happy to talk about all sorts of things from politics to literature. She was an intelligent, sensitive, articulate person who expressed deep gratitude as well as enthusiasm for our conversations. Even more impressive was that she refused to be bitter or angry because of her situation but was positive, laughed much and retained her hopes for the future—that one day she would get into a wheelchair to get herself back into the world outside. She told me that she enjoyed our times together because I did not simply see her as someone to "be done to"—a physical body only—to be fed, washed, given medication. Other aspects of her identity came alive when we made things together and chatted about what was going on in the world as well as her own hopes and dreams for the future. And I have always found that faith usually comes along at some point in a pastoral conversation, like the surprise but expected birthday cake at the end of a meal. I am never phased by this and try to always take the opportunity if the quest seems genuine, trying to position my response so it opens up rather than shuts down someone's spiritual life.

In whatever form it takes, I have always enjoyed the privilege of visiting people in their homes over the years. The instant access the collar seems to have, the fact that trust is so easily accepted as part of this. Whether there is purpose to it—to explain a baptism, to run through a wedding, to listen to another's grief, to allow an important story to unfold, or simply to get to know someone over a cup of tea, the presence of someone who has decisively made an effort to be there signifies that the other person matters. Matters and is worth taking time and trouble over. Plus the fact that our stories, whatever they might be, are never over.

It begins with an apple

Every student summer I returned to Somerset and each September of those holidays I became a seasonal worker at a nearby fruit farm. Arriving early often in crisp mist, I left in warmth, as that month's balmy sunshine burned through a cold dawn. That experience built physical resilience as I worked up to picking one and a half tons of shiny apples and rough-skinned pears of old English variety every day for three weeks plus an eight-mile round cycle trip to get there. Many days of autumnal sun were spent reaching up to pick those fruit or spent grappling about the fallen "pick-ups" as these were used for cider. The activity was solitary, like a spiritual journey; my only companions the four foremen who moved my wooden bin up and down the grassy aisles between the rows, with their tractors. I loved this outdoor life, having enjoyed reading Thomas Hardy, and this experience gave me a sense of being absorbed in a temporary rural family in a season of autumnal fruitfulness.

These days in church life, community is created best in natural, often temporary ways too. Yesterday in my jungled woodland garden we held an afternoon tea, a meal which has become very popular once again. Church folk, and their hangers-on, know how to eat. Food is provided on most occasions and a friend I know, as well as being a wizard with accounts, is a hidden and masterful baker. Baking, he tells me, is a completely different discipline to financial analysis and one which provides the satisfaction of instant results which can be enjoyed by all.

Over two and a half hours, through my garden gate trooped a multitude of people. Those I have known from before when I lived in this city, new people invited and some guests from a local organization which supports those seeking asylum and permanent home in the UK. There were kids and children of friends of parishioners visiting the area. We dusted off the croquet set and organized a treasure hunt. We have two congregations in my current parish, and the eternal old church chestnut of encouraging people to mix happened that afternoon in unselfconscious ways. I began the afternoon humping tables and chairs over from the church hall; Jean provided tablecloths and decorated jars with fresh flowers. There were, despite inevitable anxiety experienced every time we do this, enough homemade cakes to feed the five thousand.

Conscientious clergy feel an ache of responsibility at these events— they want to make sure everyone is happy, worried that no one is left out especially those who have braved it because they are new or on the edge of the inner circle. My inner extravert went into overdrive as I bobbed around, "pressing the flesh", having snatched conversations about not very much, with all and sundry. And then the moment when, scanning the scene, I stepped back into a realization of my own ridiculous irrelevance, knowing that all was well, and our good and wonderful people were themselves welcoming the stranger all in their own peculiar ways. As the event drew to a close, expressions of gratitude began as the unspoken and mysterious beauty of being a flexibly welcoming community was recognized. All I had done was to provide the garden and be there, amongst it all. Like my orchard fathers in Somerset the event and all that it offered was unpretentious but utterly full of kindness.

I chose this life partly because I love people in all their variety and craziness. The church still holds the potential for a very wide circle of people to come together to form community and establish friendships with those they might not otherwise have chosen. We know too, post-pandemic, that the effort and experience of being physically together means an experience of nuanced humanity, a blushing face, skin wrinkles in laughter, a pause in a moment when we sense another's pain, the smell of another's perfume, a tiny tattoo. Virtual companionship is always a second but sometimes easy choice. Pope Francis put it succinctly when he comments that after a gorging on networking a sense of fraternity has slipped away:

> In today's world, the sense of belonging to a single human
> family is fading, and the dream of working together for justice
> and peace seems an outdated utopia. What reigns instead is a

cool, comfortable, and globalized indifference, born of deep
disillusionment concealed behind a deceptive illusion: thinking
that we are all powerful. Isolation and withdrawal into one's
own interests are never the way to restore hope and bring about
renewal. Rather, it is closeness; it is the culture of encounter.
Isolation, no; closeness, yes.*

Many believe we are growing more distant from one another; we often
do not know who our neighbours are and as life becomes more and more
frantic, consumed with things to keep us "safe", energy to take time *with*
people feels more and more of an effort unless we know them really
well. Remaining in our safe "bubbles" (another ironic term of pandemic
leftover) means that many are left out. The church of the future is one
such place which at its very core tries to prise open this newly ingrained
attitude, to provide contexts and occasions which are genuinely open,
where we can reconnect and rediscover social delight as we acknowledge
that something deep within us all is satisfied when we know our need
of each other.

We are told by developmental psychologists that there is a staged
process with regards to learning how to love. We begin with our family
group in whatever form that might take, and some never move on from
this, simply because the love is not evident or cannot be expressed. For
the emotionally healthy, we move beyond this to love people who "feel
like us". The third stage is to develop a sense of love for people who do
not feel like us at all. Then a shut-down can happen as that step feels too
much like hard work, or too frightening as we lay aside the challenge
and scuttle back into the safety of our burrows. But this can breed an
unhealthiness, both individually but also more widely as the roots of
nationalism, a fear of "the other", or what feels like a merciless inability
to empathize in the plight of another's misfortune succeeds in public
consciousness often fuelled by the media.

But running through the Bible are stories which ask people to move
away from their own parochial boundaries to a more expansive vision.

---

*   Pope Francis, *Fratelli Tutti: On Fraternity and Social Friendship* (Huntingdon,
       IN: OSV Publishing Division, 2020), pp. 25–26.

Acts 10, for example, has Peter, often regarded as the founder of "the Church", believing that Jesus' message was just for the Jewish people. Slowly the realization dawns that he is being led to the edges of the confines of his understanding of love as God's Spirit leads him to a whole new understanding for his life, of love founded and fostered through anyone. God, it seems, shows no partiality.

As priest, I relish organizing new events which bring people together. I have the ideas and play my part in setting these up, and I am lucky as others often "catch the vision" and do the practicalities. In early July we held our main Sunday service outside, billing it as a Celebration of Creation. And people really came to have their pets blessed (a dubious theological act for some in holy orders, although not for me). We brought our slightly bemused cat (Leopold), Vicky brought hers (Kipling) sans cat carrier, on the No 50 bus, but it was Budge, our Church Warden's tortoise, who stole the show. When it came to it, I glided round our colourful gathering, blessing hamsters and dogs but also images of pets that had been too much to physically bring. I reminded our gathering that our pet friends often have unspoken pastoral gifts, sensing our moods and needs, providing companionship, opportunities for making friends on the morning walk and an appreciation of a growing sacredness in all things. Our sleepy Sunday neighbours watched over the churchyard wall and the sun came out despite worry over initial foreboding clouds. Again, new people came, seeing the service advertised: All are welcome.

When you are young, you feel a sense of loss through death or loneliness acutely. In my case, the death of a close friend through the kick of a horse, the devastation of the knowledge that a man for whom I had fallen at university had no romantic interest in me were two of these. Church communities, whether they have short or longer lifespans, do not protect us from the experiences life deals. But they have the capacity to offer a balm which soothes through a genuinely offered compassion and with this, the opportunity to have the stories of our own limits, heard. At their best, they may give us the courage to unlock our hearts again when we may have become hesitant to do so. I love this quote from Louise Eldrich's novel *The Painted Drum*:

Life will break you. Nobody can protect you from that, and being alone will not either, for solitude will also break you with its yearning. You have to love. You have to feel. It is the reason you are here on earth. You have to risk your heart. You are here to be swallowed up. And when it happens that you are broken, or betrayed, or left, or hurt, or death brushes too near, let yourself sit by an apple tree and listen to the apples falling all around you in heaps, wasting their sweetness. Tell yourself that you have tasted as many as you could.*

---

*   Louise Eldrich, *The Painted Drum* (New York: HarperCollins, 2005), p. 274.

1 9

Morning Prayer

Morning Prayer is one of the daily "offices", or forms of liturgical prayer, clergy promise to say each day in their vows at their ordination, the day they commit themselves to a life in holy orders. For centuries many clergy have said Morning as well as Evening Prayer—usually in church. For years people also attended Matins (another word for Morning Prayer) on Sundays and recited the words from the Book of Common Prayer written (and revised several times) during the English Reformation. Many churches still use this form of service (known as BCP) written primarily by Thomas Cranmer in an often-early Sunday service. But saying Morning Prayer on weekdays as a practice has dwindled with many being pressed for time, snatching a few moments to formulate their own quiet space, to say prayers or none at all, and often in their own home. Thanks to newer religious communities, whose resources are often accessible online, other creative variations have also emerged, short liturgies such as Prayer during the Day and Midday Prayer. Compline or Night Prayer is another form of prayer based on the traditional monastic rhythm of prayer over a twenty-four-hour period. In our parish, we say Morning Prayer four times a week (Friday is everyone's day-off), but Evening Prayer remains privately said, except on Sunday when this is sung as Evensong, twice a month. The following is a description of a period in my own church's life when we had formed quite a community around this office.

They wander in. A sweet and tattered group. Tall Martin, elderly and newly arrived back from abroad. He is retired clergy and disillusioned with what he describes to be "the institutionalization" of the Church. I don't quite know what he means by this, but I sense it is something about bureaucracy crushing the dynamism out of what a church community could be about. But coming to Morning Prayer seems to satisfy something he needs. He cannot hear well and so I shout instructions for where today's Psalm is to be found. Like most contemporary pilgrims we travel through the service on our phones and this, as for so many older people, is a frustration for him as the screen slips onto tomorrow's prayer and he is left lost. He carries an eccentricity and an aliveness—battered hat and russet-coloured trousers, often forgetful but off afterwards to his dance class. He holds, like so many who have participated in a lifelong ministry, firm views of how things should be done. He wants to discuss the morning's Bible commentary—it has missed the point apparently. I do not have time this morning or energy, but secretly I treasure this aliveness of his inner life, the fact he still cares in the sea that forms so much disillusionment. I wonder whether my colleagues disagree, seeing in him a rebellion that needs to be squashed, a threat which disrupts the controlled way things are done here. But to me, it is miraculous that he, and in fact all of them seek to begin their day like this, in a bone-cold church.

Mark is already here. He has grown up with the church community and is one of its stalwarts, a young member of our ever-burgeoning choir as he found an identity. He is the "site manager"—cleaner, maintenance organizer, ever-vigilant to blocked drains and gathering used needles in the churchyard, that hidden work that people beyond the community forget has to be regularly done. Mark is also manager of our public-facing ministry—posting events and successes on our Facebook page and a Reader—someone who offers their time for free, leading some services, preaching, offering pastoral care. Mark is a deeply loved member of our church and immensely gifted at just "being with" a wide variety of people. His silent presence absorbs much need which walks through our doors and sometimes he cannot understand why he is so necessary, seeing only all that he is not. It is what makes him so beautiful—those natural people with an inability to clothe himself in self-esteem and ego. They are rare in church leadership.

Now Eira arrives, young and composed in her black puffer jacket. Bespectacled and serene she reminds me of a young nun. I do not know her story, bar that at one time in her recent life coming to church proved a comfort to her. I hold myself back, adjusting to who she is, like a fine-tuning of a clock, gently but unobtrusively welcoming, pushing to the back of my mind that incredulity which asks again why a young student would choose to be here.

Ukrainian Lara shuffles in—heart of gold with constant earache. Like Martin, she cannot hear much. And Dan who lives with her has taken shelter in a house because he needed a place to live. Morning Prayer is only half an hour, but these two arrive halfway through. Some of us jump to help, rustling books, loudly stating the page numbers but somehow, they manage to join in with the remainder of the service, then wander out again.

And Leila too, Iraqi, well-spoken and pretty—a doctor. Decked out in running gear she brings her small daughter who gurgles and beams throughout the service. She is always so encouraging and warm—on a personal journey into faith I think—but life and kids and professional responsibilities crowd in even though there is so much of God in all of that. And Elisabeth, 87 and thin as a wire, one of the parish's saints. We all know it, sense it through her shaky frailty. She never stops, a blue-stockinged single lady of gargantuan character. She has been a missionary in Africa and remains ever passionate about all that is unjust; she badgers me constantly, checking about this or that charitable work and what we are doing about it. Like most saints she approaches difference with relish rather than suspicion, just as well in this multi-cultural city. During lockdown she joined with others in her block of flats, often of a different faith, over the phone, praying for those who suffered most, yearning to support those carrying the most. Through her tremulous voice we all sense a lost vision of saving the world from itself, simply, in old-fashioned unselfishness. She is wonderful as they all are.

And so, this is us, our clear-sighted, capable curate fresh from school drop off and weary vicar who sits silently, surveying this scene as well, wait for everyone to settle, a gathering which expands and shrinks every day. Last week a new person arrived, unexpectedly, her husband being in the city for health reasons. Used to this "office" because she said it regularly in her home church, this is the power of communally understood prayer in the C of E. These rituals still hold power in their rhythm, their ancient and comforting sentiments. Yet for me, my own spirituality moves at a tangent with what I do here each morning as I seek often now a quieter, more contemplative solace. For this beginning is far from peaceful for me and that is the honest truth. But my calling here is to join and lead others into the rare tranquillity that will settle their souls for this day. I often do not feed my own spirituality in this way anymore—Morning Prayer—the way we do it anyhow—is too disjointed, disrupted, too exhausting, coping with the inclusion of all these good folk. Yet the day begins, and faithfulness continues, people and the world prayed for, and God listens anyway.

2 0

"Say one for me"—Heartfelt requests

"Say one for me," Father (only I'm not), but the desire is there. A reaching out to he or she who is understood to have a hotline to heaven to ask God something important on their behalf. Good theology should replace bad perhaps. Why would God open his ears anymore to me if God loves all humanity exactly the same? I am apparently more integrated into things of holiness and mystery. But I never stop to argue when someone asks that but just respond with love, "Of course I will," I say. It is a reaching out and connection made. We pray for lives dilapidated and hurting, and that moment of encounter is a kind of holding.

People who have no faith pray. Prayer is not a shopping list hurled at some power "out there" we hope might deliver us what we passionately want. Prayer is for me a stepping down or into some kind of mystery and peace I know I will never completely understand but which I can sense intuitively. It is as though there is a realm embodied in the air we breathe which fuses with the earthly and ordinary life that we live, of ironing and laughter, busy streets and astonishing architecture. Prayer has changed over the years, in practice as well as in understanding, and like many experiences of solace and transcendence has different facets. It is an antidote to worry, it is, like a vigilante, the reminder of the pains and passions of others, and of how I can ease that by some contribution of recognition. It is the sensing of another way when we need to draw on an otherworldly largesse to overcome our inability to pull ourselves out of a state of mind or situation. At times of desperation in my life I have hammered on the doors of God's guesthouse, wanting to know I can be let in from the storm.

But I don't know what I believe about praying. I like to believe that somehow my small effort makes a difference to someone, somewhere.

That sentiment or request offered in heartfelt sincerity can be placed in a metaphorical bottle and sent to where it is needed to be poured out to soothe and stop and cure. Healing or peace, food, or companionship. God and angels do some heavenly sorting in the post office in the sky and direct those prayers to the right mailbox. It could be so. Others tell me they pray for me, and it makes me feel held and loved; it is a faithfulness of sorts. Prayer is modelled as a one-way street on Sunday mornings on the whole and some of my congregation do this expertly, carefully crafted words of nuance and the pause which allows those words to touch the heart. It is the beginning of believing a better future into being. Here is a dreaming of a different world that could be built.

Faisal Mohyuddin has written the most achingly beautiful poem about prayer, that here is routine and ritual which clears the debris we collect in heart and mind each day, to place ourselves within the waterfall of God's energy and light. There is a porous nature to good prayer, power flows in as anxieties, control, ego flow out. The author writes without punctuation and in five stanzas where there are physical gaps on the written page, as though the poem itself becomes a metaphor of the space that prayer can create. The poem describes the rituals of preparing the body for prayer in the Islamic tradition where people of faith pray five times every day. Before one even begins there is a slowing down, an attempt for the mind to filter the detritus accumulated and for mental clutter to literally "un-fasten", to slow.

Prayer for me gathers in a myriad of emotions, depending on what the day holds. Prayer is everything that matters, a kaleidoscope which colours life with a richness which infuses the rest of the day. Every time that happens each configuration is different, and there is hope in that. Prayer becomes the recognition that in a tiny observed moment there is something eternal seen or heard or touched which bears a light and a love which will not die.

My Anglican tradition loves words too. Words we call liturgy, often words said over and over, and which can sump down like sustained nutrition. We live through the voices of those who have cried or praised before us, in desperate longing or in joyful gratitude as our words flow into the prayers of the saints and martyrs over centuries. So many words for me become prayer now. I know they are so when I hear them, the words of *Desiderata* for example, not a traditional "prayer" or belonging to any faith as such but words which contain a universality and a resonance which connects with what we feel to be healthy, and right. This poem by Max Ehrman communicates above all, a balance. It concludes:

> And whether it is clear to you, no doubt the universe is unfolding as it should. Therefore, be at peace with God, whatever you conceive Him to be. And whatever your labours and aspirations, in the noisy confusion of life, keep peace in your soul. With all its sham, drudgery and broken dreams, it is still a beautiful world. Strive to be happy.

What could be more contemporary or universal as prayer?

Over the years I have moved a thousand miles in terms of this mystery we call prayer. From necessary childhood mantras which embed the idea of someone watching over us I said every night in my bedroom:

> Matthew, Mark, Luke and John,
> Bless the bed that I lie on.
> Four corners to my bed,
> Four angels round my head.
> One to watch and one to pray,
> and two to bear my soul away.

That feels twee now, but I grew up as an only child in a fearsome and draughty vicarage. Terror in those 23 rooms was real when I was small. I listened to the gentle beauty of the Psalms, sung at Evensong, as I knelt on the wooden floor of my father's stall in a darkened cathedral. I have learnt and then taught others to read the Bible stories and then to imagine them in their minds, often with unpredictable results as Christ speaks directly to each pilgrim. I have practised the Examen as the day lived is rewound, in all its balm and boredom, to try to glimpse where the movement of the divine was felt in this embodied world. I have practised prayers of breath and silence, wafted incense and lit a thousand candles. But recently there has felt to be an arrival (not a destination) at a place where I draw from a silent well of otherness I know not where it has come from. It is, I think, an acknowledgment of the sacredness at the heart of us all, flowers at the centre of everything. It is an understanding that the whole of our lives can be understood as some kind of strange panoptical and living prayer. And increasingly I like people who I can be quiet with. Words still matter but they can no longer invoke the mystery I wish to stay within.

In every house we lived in throughout my childhood, my mother created a space to pray in—her *poustinia* at the bottom of the garden, a chapel under the eaves of a much smaller house, a "pod" she bought in retirement and had erected in a tiny yard in her Welsh home. These were spaces where she could recite the traditional prayers of the church, be restored, think about others, tend to the spiritual part of herself in private, to seek life at depth uninterrupted. For my mother here was a place where she made sense of the world. A place of listening and occasionally asking. A place of establishing and residing. A place where the madness is removed and the realization grows that everything is spiritual and the way we understand prayer to "work" is mostly infantile. A place where we hold onto what gives us life. Like her now I need that solace to keep practising love. Prayer is an undoing of ego.

Vivek Murthy, US Surgeon General, offers four practices for sustaining our spiritual life, one of which is the practice of "wasting" time. Many of us tend no longer to do this as we use every waking moment efficaciously. We work through our in-boxes as we wait on the train platform rather than just waiting on the platform to give our minds and hearts a chance to drain of ceaseless thought. We need the chance to recover from the stress and energy within life, to dwell with questions and to allow silence to restore our punctured depths.*

---

* Podcast "To be a healer"—interview with Krista Tippet, On Being project, 13 April 2023.

2 1

Wilderness

February is wilderness time. It is still cold, the vain exhilaration of Christmas gone, and spring not quite arrived. A month of love or often the lack of it as Valentine's Day lies in the middle. It is the time in the church year when Lent usually begins too, the six-week, forty-day season which still resides in the consciousness of the public as people tell me what they are going to give up or take up. After a lifetime of giving things up, my own resistance to this kind of sacrifice feels immense, as I, rightly or wrongly, now revel a little in my complete lack of discipline. I try to live more frugally, to pray more, be more patient, encourage the congregation into a challenge, but mostly miserably fail.

I like the story of Jesus going into the desert to be tested by Satan. It is an eerie yet substantial tale of the loneliness of the fight within, as the Son of God manages to get his appetites in check by not eating for 40 days and by pushing back the opportunity to become both a powerful leader and a charismatic miracle worker. I imagine him surrounded by the bleakness of infinity-horizons, shouting back at, and into nothing, slowly thinking he is going mad. There is no one to love here and the temptation to love himself alone in inappropriate ways must be withheld. There is nothing to do but begin to count the grains of sand, the odd scorpion his only companion.

Some years ago, I visited Dungeness—a triangular area of land that juts out into the sea—Kent's most southerly point—and shaped so due to the movement of the tide pressing into the peninsula from both directions. If you look out to sea from this, one of Europe's largest shingle beaches, you can see for yourself the movements of the waves. Dungeness feels a strange, end-of-the-world type place. Disused railway carriages from the 1920s and other beach shacks have been converted into permanent or holiday-type clapboard dwellings by local anglers or working people anxious to escape the pressured environment of London. The artist and film director Derek Jarman's Prospect Cottage remains an important historical landmark, complete with its sculptures made from his beach-combing finds. Dungeness is a Marmite place—you either love it or hate it. Visiting it during a summer holiday in 2020, I loved it's other-worldly quirkiness, the abandoned boats on the shore with their peeling paint, set under a vast expanse of azure sky. It felt somewhere a person might come to escape, to think, or to hide, a place neither here nor there, edgy and elemental, like the American frontier of the eighteenth century.

The wilderness is often a place of vast space and big skies. Yet within such vastness there is the irony of claustrophobia—somewhere a person is strangely contained as there feels to be no borders, no boundaries, a place where entry and exit are not easily discernible. In the Bible, Psalm 63 talks of travelling across dry and weary deserts to reintegrate an experience of God which then becomes a place of reorientation and a pathway out. Spiritual deserts can happen unexpectedly as we feel picked up, as if by a fairground claw, and dumped in the middle of a void for whatever reason. There is a deep disorientation as our normal points of references are removed from us—employment, status, security and, at times, love. But wilderness is part of our human condition.

The recent pandemic has proved to be such an experience as normal privileges and securities were stripped away from many a life, and often suddenly. Individuals working in companies for decades found themselves redundant at the wrong time of life, leaving them floundering, not knowing where to turn with mortgages still to pay. The Church was anxious too, the post-Christian wilderness it has found itself in, accentuated with anxiety about returning numbers, loss of income and simply not knowing how to operate safely in an organization that prides itself on its interaction with people and the building of community. Yet here was also opportunity—to revision how a faith community might work in the future, what forms and norms it could create as people search for a new way of spiritual expression and understandings of God, even if this meant dispensing and letting go of some of the things which are held dear—buildings, status, policy, financial security.

At Dungeness, there remain physical symbols of what has held past power and accomplishment, and which are now redundant—one of the lighthouses and a power station. These remain part of the significance and history of this area. But replacements have been built and life, as well as beauty abound in the new simplicity of the reconditioned shacks, some of which also house art galleries. Innovation and a new sense of ownership are working themselves out in this desert space too.

Great richness can be found in the desert too. A past summer in Morocco I discovered it in the nuances of sunset and sunrise, the grey lumps of humphing camels who made a solid ring of protection around our night-time camp. The richness of the Amazigh culture, vibrant in its nomadic glory—colourful carpets laid down and sweetness of welcome from dates and tea. Wilderness is sometimes described as No Man's Land—an analogy suggesting that the land belongs to no one either because it is too vast, too wild, too uncontained or because no one has claimed it yet.

Many of these themes did not go unnoticed by Jarman himself who spent the latter part of his life dedicated to gay rights issues as he was diagnosed as HIV positive. Within the desert conditions of Dungeness, Jarman established a beautiful garden, helped by friends with horticultural expertise, using local plants that would thrive. They collected old fishing tackle, shells and broken driftwood to construct sculptures, many of which still stand at Prospect Cottage. It became for him a place of solace where he drew great richness out of desolation as well as disillusionment—he used the area as the setting for several of his films. Particularly powerful is *The Garden* (1990) which focuses on the experience and oppression of being gay in an era when HIV/AIDS was in the forefront of society's consciousness and as an issue, often misunderstood and judged accordingly. The film has strong Christian associations, connecting these to what it meant to be gay in the twentieth century and highlighting Section 28 which Jarman strongly opposed. He became increasingly disenchanted, as many also were during the Thatcher-years, witnessing the growing emphasis on material wealth as well as the diminishment of traditional working industries such as mining. Dungeness as wilderness was symbolic of the bleakness he felt within his personal life and the idea of love withheld from a society wrestling to dispense with longstanding and conservative notions of sexuality.

I visited Dungeness at a time in my life where I felt professionally and spiritually exposed and when the love and loyalty of the institution, which had felt like a trusted friend, suddenly withdrew its shelter. I felt judged unfairly and misunderstood and where I was flicked out, all too easily like a suddenly menacing insect. When love is withheld swiftly and cruelly, as it was for me by those who held ecclesial power, the only company remaining came from the depths of oneself. There was a deep dive into the abyss of what my life was meant to be about, with the stubborn refusal to believe there would be no way out of that frightening and unknown place I had found myself in. It felt like the beginning of a new way of living, somehow more elemental, riskier with a more trust-filled spirituality. My own trusty band of disciples were those who refused to demonize, knowing and understanding how a person can find themselves in such a place. Dungeness became a place of profound symbolism, and it was here I drew on divine power, pulling up new energy to guide and protect what I had left of my professional life. The innovation and creativity symbolized in the transformation of redundant spaces and sheds in that place, the fragile natural life living well in bees and insects was a taste of honey on the lips and a path in hope.

But time moves on and now, in another era, wilderness falls upon me only occasionally, shocking me awake like a house alarm in the night. That year, the horizon opened as I found my way out into a new role through the giving of a second chance from someone who had been there himself. Trekking onwards, out of unrelenting desolation to a kindlier oasis, that time now mostly vanishes like a mirage. There, in the wilderness of failure, emerged a strange and new journey without direction.

2 2

Grief

I am on the other side of grief. My mother, after a battle with bowel cancer, passed away in a local hospice last year. I took her funeral—a strange mixture of the personal and professional, as I felt the weight of responsibility to respect her wishes. She wanted me to officiate at the service and to be buried with my father in the Southwest, in a cemetery overlooking blue hills. My family made food for those who had travelled long distances to be in the tiny country church which had been her parish. To the amusement of the undertakers, we decided to transport her body ourselves, all the way to Somerset. But that quirkiness felt authentic to who she was, a stoic woman of strong faith, who got the cobwebs down from her cottage two weeks before she died, joking that death was taking its time.

We were there when she passed from this world to another realm somewhere. I am meant to know where that is, but at this moment I'm not sure. In the chair I sobbed, a nurse kneeling before me, holding my hand, gently trained to "just be". We left the room for a while and on return the simple gesture of a fresh flower had been placed on my mum's pillow. I cried not just for that moment but for a thousand strange things which emerge from within us when we understand that life has changed irreversibly. It had been just her and me for over 35 years—intense often. The last ten years had been peaceful between us, and I, growing up into a happy plateau of maturity, suddenly stopped blaming her for the scars of my youth. That had been replaced by a new insight into her, the sacrifices made, frugality lived, the lack of fuss at inconvenience or physical discomfort.

Since her passing, I have lived mostly in a reconstructed elegy, her life intricately bound up with all my memories, places I have lived, significant moments of celebration and crisis, which she lived through too. And I cried in the knowledge that I will never hear her voice again save on an ansaphone message on my mobile. "Grief does not obey your plans, or your wishes. Grief will do whatever it wants to you, whenever it wants to. In that regard, Grief has a lot in common with Love," so says Elizabeth Gilbert.*

And that is true. Grief is also highly individual. It has made me tired, nostalgic, anxious. It has made me plough on amidst the hard work of funeral organizations and the return to a crisis in my parish. But I am so fortunate for I am surrounded by the instant balm of loving kindness of hugs and cards and understanding as well as respect that I have chosen to still show up on Sundays.

Recently a few of us have participated in a bereavement course which aims to support people living with the heartbeat of grief. It has been excellent, but I and one other participant have voiced concerns, feeling like imposters, believing we have not really experienced the death of someone close ourselves. I lost my father when I was 17 but simply got on with my A-levels. Years later I sobbed my heart out unexpectedly in a dark cinema as grief overtook in resonances of the subject of the film which had been about the close relationship of a daughter and her father. Exhausted, my heart wrung out, I left feeling like something that had been buried way down deep had been dug up, dislodged.

I hope now to offer the training received as a gentle open space to anyone who is desperately missing someone who cannot be glimpsed or touched any longer. The course taught us to give time, to be patient, to allow grief to take its course and to not rush sadness. There is no right way to grieve but to help someone to do it as they need to, for that is to provide a sanctuary. There are people in our community who have lost spouses of over 50 years. There are young women who have lost tiny babies. There are members of my family who have lost young men to suicide and to cancer way before their time was up. They carry that pain like silt which settles but is sometimes stirred up when jolted by a word or smell or anniversary. There is life before a loved one and life after they have gone.

---

* Elizabeth Gilbert, quoted in Brene Brown, *Atlas of the Heart* (London: Vermillion/Penguin Random House, 2021), p. 110.

That fact never changes, and it is only what we choose to do with it that can enable there to be some tranquillity and emotional equilibrium; grief in different levels of intensity simply becomes part of us.

Grief affects so many of us, as Gilbert suggests. It has no mercy or predictability, save that it rises and falls. Because of this the church community has an opportunity to provide a place for people to be real within it and to be soothed, even if this is a temporary haven. But sanctuary comes in other ways too. Growing up in Cornwall, walking on expansive beaches contemplating the ocean became one of those for me. The sea, that mysteriously powerful symbol of universality taught me much. The faithfulness of life's dynamic in its waves which roll up in the tide each day; life goes on, this time will pass as the old saying goes. That we are part of something bigger than ourselves; the horizon tells us that. That absorbing the atmosphere of being at the coast, whether cove or cliff, strangely rinses us through with a surety of a future. Others walk and walk and walk, pacing grief out, creating pilgrimages of desolation as well as healing. Others talk, and talk, talking it out with priests, or counsellors, or friends, or others who have been there and never seem to get bored of hearing the same repeated story.

And then there is other grief. Loss that should not be so hard hitting but stamps itself onto who we are, like a badly applied tattoo, labelling us as tainted or failures and redirecting our future. Our dreams of who we might have been, the possibility of professional success or personal happiness, poisoned. I have met many who have been dispensed with in their jobs, put outside the camp like rubbish no longer needed, only to spend years recovering from the rejection. Many too have never salvaged their wrecked hearts after resignation or when a spouse leaves or when a parent refuses to sew up a hurt.

Clerics absorb pain most of the time. We must be ready for it, like the curved ball thrown from the side. We must be careful with it too, with our words, our sincerity, our way of understanding God. Jesus was always attentive when he encountered grief and pain. People say to me now, "Be gentle with yourself", and they are right. For now, it is the clearing out of a life, a life intricately bound up with mine. Everything weighty with memory, from towels with holes to old pots my mother cooked with from when I was a child. Never have I had to take such care, out of respect for a lifetime of keeping things. Now her things will be assimilated in mine, a disjunct with more recent stuff and oblivious to the power they hold. For every time I open the wooden chest, or wear that ring, or wash up the bowl, it will jolt her life back to life through the memories of what has been. In remembering we put back together those precious things which no one else shares—those sweet or sour times from former years.

Navigating grief for others remains a major domain for clergy. But diving into my own was a sharp reminder that there is no room ever to become blasé. I wrote my mother's eulogy and was proud of that honouring. Family and I created the service with exceptional care. It has reminded me that even though I may go through the same questions with a bereaved person I must take time to listen, to be patient as those who grieve are often so achingly tired they cannot think straight. From grief too emerges the big questions. In my own family we have asked those too, the prepackaged faith answers of what happens after we die having disappeared down the road long ago. My daughter asked whether we thought Granny was now reunited with Grandad. I asked them whether they thought my mum could now somehow "see" all the things I never told her about my life. We pondered what kind of heaven my mother might now reside in and how that tallied with the kind of heaven we might want to live eternally in as well. We found no answers, but it felt good in the wondering. And comfort is found in remembering. The dead are only dead when we forget them.

My experience has taught me that honesty leads to a sense of authenticity when we are unsure of how to respond to questions or emotions. I also start with what I believe, setting aside the things I am meant to say. Those who are grieving can smell the rat of insincerity and sanctimony a mile away. But they recognize me as someone of theological expertise and who has thought carefully about these matters of mystery. Although I want to honour that, I am still not always sure what I think about resurrection and how that is meant to happen but that is the nature of faith. But what I do say is that human beings are too important for death to be the end of a life.

In terms of unanswered questions, Jesus as a leader did not fall into the trap of providing definitive answers. Instead, he connected past, present and future through referencing history, observing the present and pointing (often enigmatically) to the future using metaphor and story, giving those questioning space to think it out for themselves. Being comfortable and kind with unanswered questions is part of a brave priest's response to people who are grieving as well as searching through the fog of loss and its sibling emotions of anger, anxiety and confusion.

If we grieve much it is because we have also loved much. And most of us would, if it were a choice not to feel so devastated when someone we love dies, still choose to have loved that person. In grief, we are often kept going, through a long recovery, because of the warmth of others, those who are stalwarts in our lives as well as finding empathy in more unexpected places. We discover God in the sanctuary of a beating heart as well as the promise of spring.

Wise friends

It takes a long time to grow an old friend

(For Jane)

Companion on the way.
It takes a long time to grow an old friend.
Over the years our paths have been
Both certain and uncontemplated.
You saved me from an unhappy house at 19.
I stepped into the story of your life as you did mine.
You saved all your cash for those green shoes in Venice.
I hold my memories.
Of walking in Turkey, art galleries and food in flats.
We laughed and drank on joyful ground as well as now,
fortitude in the midst of pain
in my shaken life.
Your measure and resilience
is an inspiration.
You have magnified who I am.
Always knowing what to say and
how to be kind without a showy faith.
Knowing naturally when moments
are sacred in significance or sorrow.
And always there
in the promise of tomorrow's unfolding years.*

---

* "It takes a long time to grow an old friend" is a quote from a greetings card
Jane gave me a few years ago. I loved the way that phrase was put alongside

Priests need friends. People they can be completely themselves with. I wrote the above poem for one of my two longstanding friends. I have known Jane since university, for over 36 years. She and a gaggle of her mates provided sanctuary for me as we lived away from campus during my second year. First year students often have to choose who they will live with the following year before they really know the people they are committing to. The three girls I had signed a contract with were perfectly pleasant but in the "in crowd". Intuitively, I did not feel quite comfortable with them, so I migrated a few doors up the road, acquisitioning the couch of Jane and her three housemates. They were more than hospitable, and there began to grow friendships in which I felt much more at home.

Perhaps because the professional life of a cleric can be transient, these relationships feel especially precious. Over the years friendship has provided a special economy for me. Neither of my two best friends are people I would describe as "people of faith" in terms of them participating in the things people of faith do, but I must admit I don't recall many conversations about this over the years, it feeling somehow unnecessarily intrusive and as if I am strangely judging them. But one financially supports her local church, while the other is someone I can discourse with at depth about issues of spirituality. Friendship is perhaps the place of ultimate acceptance where we can share the intimate parts of ourselves; it goes beyond fear of reprisal or judgment because we know we are seen in all our ugliness but loved anyway. Both my closest friends are people who have steadfastly stood by me, and who I know would continue to do so. That alone offers an immense reassurance.

What makes a friendship can be a mysterious thing. Jane and I have a common starting point—we are both only children, have had to cope from an early age emotionally and financially, and have been without a father since childhood. We have shared a flat in Venice, been on holiday to Turkey, talked and laughed through our lives with philosophy and

---

the image of an oak tree, reminding me too of the steadfast character of Gabriel Oak in one of my favourite Thomas Hardy novels, *Far from The Madding Crowd*. I wrote the poem at a time in my life when I felt particularly appreciative of my closest friendships.

relish, sharing memories as well as an ongoing love of life, art and good food. I deeply respect everything she is and what she has achieved.

Making friends in a parish situation is inevitably tricky, and different clergy have different rules. It potentially blurs pastoral boundaries as well as encouraging jealousy from others who might wonder why they are not in favour. But over the years I have tried not to be too precious about this, because inevitably there are people with whom we feel a deep kinship for whatever reason. My personality type tells me I naturally seek deep and sustained friendships of meaning. And there seems nothing worse than a standoffish leader who never makes themselves vulnerable, refusing hospitality, set apart and above everyone else in terms of their own emotional needs. Clergy can be lonely and vulnerable too, and often the reality is there is precious little extra time to sustain relationships outside of a ministerial context, like some other professions too. That context often tends to feel all-encompassing, and it feels natural to make friends with people who are near, or that we feel drawn too or who offer their support. I have gathered several close friends along the way, even though I do not live geographically close any more. And sometimes friendship or simply "being friendly" goes wrong; we send out the wrong messages, we accept gifts we should not accept, and occasionally people become angry or fixated with clerical figures. It can be confusing for people to understand where the professional line is drawn as well as why we need to withdraw into a more private world.

Good friendship is non transactional, refreshes the spirit and allows us to become absorbed into another's world for a little where there are no agendas. I love visiting my other best friend, Jacques, committed vegan and hardworking nurse of nights, who has adopted ten-year-old Jess (that fact itself a sanctuary) and lives in a cottage in the country with two dogs, a cat and some chickens. We grew up together in Cornwall and spent many childhood holidays together, dreaming about boys and smoking furtive cigarettes on the pebbled beaches on hidden coves. You know a good friend when they change their rotas, organize childcare, stay overnight to attend your mother's funeral.

At times of sustained crisis and suffering in my life I have often appreciated the etymology of the other word for friend—companion— defined as "a friend who is frequently in the company of another". For

Christians who pray this "company" can mean a spiritual "being with", when physical distance means we cannot meet face-to-face. Strong friendship involves a quality of conversation, which seeks the truth of things, is honest about who we are and dismisses all sense of falsity and façade. After they had experienced his ministry, committed to following him and were beginning to understand the nature of what he was called to do, Jesus says to his friends, in John's Gospel, "I do not call you servants any longer, because the servant does not know what the master is doing; but I have called you friends, because I have made known to you everything that I have heard from my father." (John 15:15)

Jane, Jacques and some others among my friends also introduce a deeper element to this reflection. They are naturally endowed with the ability to say (or not say) the right (or the wrong) thing when the conversation plumbs the depths. Pastorally they are very proficient. Through my life I had been lucky to enjoy the fruits of others' grace; those I go to to seek some kind of way forward. Good wisdom helps us to grow and to grow up as well. And Peter—mentor and champion—a friend who has re-emerged in my life just at the right time, offering his gravitas, experience, and passion for justice, in both world and church. I met Peter when I was in my twenties. Previous roles have taken him into many scenarios and around the world, conversing and listening to people which enable them to make the right decisions at the right time whatever that might mean. Listening to such a variety of cultural expressions of faith and community means that listening to him is always a rich and valuable experience.

And locally there is one I share food and conversation with. We share an integral understanding of a sense of the divine in a metaphorical place as we grasp at the insufficiency of words. So, we grapple, attempting to describe the experience of God in both of our lives, in ways where there is a sense of being brought full circle, a place where all is connected, where we and most other "issues" cease to matter. Here, it feels safe to express what might be conceived of as unorthodox views and where there is nothing to constrict the explorations of the spiritual. It is a special space for me in the knowledge that we share an established yet ever shifting understanding about the nature of God and how this can be expressed. It is good to know people who can expand the previous limits of our own firm beliefs as well. We talk of the things which have recently captured our hearts and souls and gently bat them around. Wisdom is hearing new truth. It is hearing the obvious from a new perspective.

Good companionship is about unadulterated faithfulness, a sticking *with* as the small band of women walked with Jesus all the way to the cross and stood by while that bitter death had passed. In the book of Ruth, Ruth and Naomi's is a friendship discovered in a challenging and unlikely place as well—through bereavement and vulnerability. Ruth refuses to leave her mother-in-law even though she has every excuse to return home to her original land. David and Jonathan's friendship is described in 1 Samuel 18, whose souls are knit together. Jonathan is unwaveringly loyal to David, warning him of King Saul's treachery. These two young men shared a close emotional bond and were unafraid to share their feelings—perhaps a timely example of the male need to do this more openly in a contemporary society where independence, employment and sexual success can feel oppressive to many. The friendship between Elijah and Elisha has at its centre the purposeful choosing of friends. Elisha sees in Elijah an excellent mentor and guide and steadfastly devotes himself to the older man until Elijah can pass on his prophetic ministry to him. Biblical companionship comes in human form.

But the strongest and archetypical metaphor of friendship for the Christian life lies within the Trinity. Here is an ever-expanding model for friendship with all people regardless of colour, class, race, faith, age, or social standing. Some of the holiest people I have known have friends who span all of these and cross the boundaries of them rather than becoming overly boundaried. It provides an example of companionship which is about a natural respect in the individuality and beauty of each person. The dynamic of Father, Son and Spirit becomes a living metaphor, enabling us to recognize that we hold a deep need for another through relationship.

2 4

Living in rest

A friend offered me the following quote from Meister Eckhart (Sermon 45) recently. It is one which has been returned to again and again as it has appeared in sermons, as a quote offered to a friend and to reflections on what it might mean to abandon ourselves to a different way of living as well as being:

> If I were asked to say to what end the Creator has
> created all creatures, I would say: rest.
> If I were asked secondly what the Holy Trinity sought
> in all its works, I would answer: rest.
> If I were asked thirdly what the soul sought in all
> her agitations, I would answer: rest.
> If I were asked fourthly what all creatures sought in their natural
> desires and motions, I would answer: rest. Amen.*

At the heart of this is the turning of tables, not only on the Protestant Work Ethic (PWE) of which many of us have been schooled in, as well as scarred by. There is the radical suggestion too, that to arrive at a place of peace with all, as well as to operate from a place of rest rather than busyness just might be the vocational purpose of our existence. The final line suggests that underneath all humanity's incessant activity there lies a nascent desire to be at peace with ourselves and the world. But the PWE told us that we must work hard to justify our existence, self-esteem, place in society. The PWE tells us that the very worst crime of all is to be

---

*   *The Complete Mystical Works of Meister Eckhart*, tr. Maurice O'C. Walsh (New York: Crossroad Publishing, 2010).

understood or misinterpreted as "lazy". Success looks like resilience in all its forms and in it, we must always stay in control.

As priest I am one of the worst offenders. After a snatched Morning Prayer (never a contemplative activity for I say this with others) I begin a busy day. These days the day often turns over one piece of ministry after another, the roller-coaster of emotions that is involved as we move from school assembly to funeral visit to church meeting, to crisis with the heating. It is the keeping in my head of all the thousand bitty pieces of detail I have to remember to do, communicate, think about or forget. It is exhausting.

"Silence is not something we make it is something we enter. It is something that is always there", said Mother Maribel of Wantage.* My friend told me not to struggle with finding a regimented time to "be quiet" but instead to allow those moments to fall upon us. To find things which create natural opportunities for us to slip into rest and to stay in its soft feathers for a while. For when this is sustained, we emerge softer and kinder for the world. Stronger too, we find more strength to resist the conflict and unpleasantness we sometimes encounter. Finding these things and those places changes too. It is for me at this time of writing the listening to a poetry podcast—lyrical, global, meditative—words and music carefully chosen, and delivered in a voice which is mesmerizing in the listening. This "space" opens a part of me which takes me beyond the tiring constraints and worries of my life.

Places operate as rest too and often catch us unaware. Places which embody a silence, a mystery, or an ambience which allow our minds and hearts to be led to a different sphere. There is a place in the Naukluft National Park in the Namibian desert called Deadvlei ("dead marsh"). It is a white clay pan which was formed after rainfall, creating temporary shallow pools where the abundance of water allowed thorn trees to grow. Climate change has meant that drought has hit the area with sand dunes encroaching on the pan, blocking the river from the area. Now, eerie, blackened trees populate its flat and dusty base like natural statues, as if silent music has suddenly ceased to play. I have visited this place, and it

---

*   Quoted in Lavinia Byrne (ed.), *The Hidden Tradition: Women's Spiritual Writings Rediscovered* (London: SPCK, 1991), p. 122.

carries a strange beauty as the charcoal trunks contrast to the red sand of some of the highest dunes in the world, tangerine orange set against an azure sky. Hot winds blow through but even these do not cut the silence.

There have been many places which have stopped me in my tracks with their intrinsic power to make us stop to sense another sphere and to contemplate. Ruthwell Church just northwest of Carlisle, where England borders Scotland, houses an ancient as well as enigmatic Anglo-Saxon cross. It is so large it is positioned in a recess below the level of the floor, and it dominates the interior. Here is not any artificial revering of the monstrance but a presence that commands a stopping to take notice of all the cross suggests. I visited this church as a young ordinand, and my mother, who had discovered it, told me, "It's quite spooky, you know." That was enough for me not to want to step inside. The cross has some unusual depictions of Christ as well as ancient Runic script around its edge. One sentence reads, "With missiles wounded, they laid him down limb-weary, they stood by him." We are wounded too, carrying around the battle scars from past and present hurts as well as a tiredness not easily shaken off because of them. The cross draws a power to visitors, even though I did indeed find it an eerie piece of stone. But it brought me to a halt, even then, at a time in my life when I had only myself to be responsible for. Then time stretched and I wasted it productively, sitting around, talking, drinking, musing on the meaning of life through faith and there was a healthiness in that. At times I yearn to rediscover that time again and somehow this cross whispered how important that was.

Operating from a place of rest goes way beyond wellbeing. It means we begin to operate differently as we cultivate more time to think more deeply about everything. And that is hard. It is impossible to do it all the time for we simply have things to do, and life erodes our harmonies through its relentless and sometimes savage ways. Rest feels like an emergency exit we can see through the darkness in a way of life which has become overly anxious. We can secretly be wedded to that too, in the way "doing things" makes us feel worthy.

Padraig O'Tuama offers a powerful example in his book *In the Shelter: Finding a Home in the World.* On an ordinary grey day, walking around Belfast he saw a woman pushing a buggy with a two-year-old child in it. As small children often are, the child was restless and complaining.

The woman stopped and walked around to the front of the pushchair and screamed at the child, "I fucking hate you." As O'Tuama noted, life went on in that street and that story was not specific to Belfast. In fact, it happened to me, as my mother told me; she had been wheeling me in a similar pushchair down a country lane in Devon one sunny afternoon when I must have been the same age. I was also crying and she, perhaps after nights of no sleep and the responsibilities of a vicar's wife, yelled "Shut up you, stupid brat." She relayed that story to me years later, with a certain sense of *schadenfreude* which shocked and hurt me at the time. Those two snapshots bring out the judge in all of us, but really they are about the breaking points we reach. And they are about the weight of the loads we carry and how unbearably heavy these can become, even if those loads contain beautiful things like children. I do not remember that encounter—I was simply too young, and I hope the other child from Belfast did not either. O'Tuama reminds his readers that to raise a child is a long-haul operation, exhausting, especially when poverty is situated in a life. It is a lesson often in failure as well as success. He concludes, "Whenever I think of the woman, I hope that in her own fury she could hear something of her own need."* The stout and kindly farmer's wife who invited my mother to a meal she did not have to cook and who had met her coming round the corner of the lane had heard something of that need as well.

My life is one for extraverts mostly. You have to like people in this job, enjoy being with them, always courteous, always have time, whoever they are. I am, like many clergy, a high performing introvert which means I appear as an extravert, but the reality is that I get very tired from too much company and intensive one-to-ones. I need to restore, a good coffee at my favourite café with its plants in vintage boxes on the walls, and on my own. I need to not feel the press of people, insistent decisions, the ongoing keeping-it-goingness of church life. As I reach the mid-point in my own life, I am also aware that even though life "out there" has speeded up over the last few decades, life inside of me needs to slow down. This could be both a definitive stance of maturity as well as an inevitable

---

*	Padraig O'Tuama, *In the Shelter: Finding a Home in the World* (London: Hodder & Stoughton, 2015), p. 96.

lessening of energy as I have little time to "build stuff up" anymore and to worry about bums on seats. I can start new ventures, put in place great ideas, and if they progress and develop church life, all to the good, but this will be incidental as opposed to any planned outcome sought.

I currently have Covid and this should be a needed opportunity for enforced rest. But I am flitting between trying to use the time of isolation to deal with emails and sort out Sunday and jet wash the drive. I must use my time well and be conscientious, but I really should be resting my sick body in a boat which has nothing else in it but the sweet time for restoration. None of us will ever arrive at the completion of the vision of rest which Meister Eckhart suggests. But this is a calling in itself. The call to have the time to look and to listen for God in spaces and in people, and when we are not dislocated or moithered. From a place of unhurried calm is where we can begin to make greater sense of the world and make a difference to it too.

2 5

Rest house

There is a place to go. I call it a village of healing. A small collection of farm buildings used to shelter animals and a converted long barn nestles in a verdant valley deep in the West Country. It can be difficult to access without a car, and where I stay is a converted pig pen and named just that. Or a hen coop. Somehow it has built a particular focus as a place of restoration and healing for tired and disillusioned clergy as well as those who have been broken by what can be a punitive and unforgiving institution. At night the air is clear and brisk, stars seen easily without the polluted light of the urban scape. Stillness begins to fill what is empty and the cold air promises a mending of the ruin of who we believe ourselves to be. Here a healing sews up the rips and soaks up the tears. Anyone can come here. In a different kind of peace from our everyday we are taken by surprise if we are open to the listening. We do not always know where we will find our rescue.

Another place I love is arrived at by a potholed muddied track and the Franciscan brothers traverse it by Land Rover. The friary at the top is cool white inside, the entrance a welcome place of homemade jam to buy and a selection of the brothers' wellies, all which says this place is holy but earthed. In my room I smell the incense from the chapel, listen to the rain and hoots from owls. It is quiet, so quiet. I love the meals here, together and simple, taken on scrubbed wooden tables with the view of looking through a picture window to an overgrown courtyard garden. A charmed place where feral cats are fed, and weeds loved.

One former catholic seminary, full of saintly statues and things which felt to me both familiar and yet strangely alien, made me want to turn around and flee. But here was the place where Gerard Manley Hopkins had become a priest, his poetry unwound for the world. That world, in the hills of North Wales with its gardens of rose blooms was where he saw the grandeur of divine glory unfolding like crinkled foil in a vision of oozing, verdant abundance. I was led in my imagination through a serious of exercises, a surprising version of Jesus speaking to me and my imagination painting new pictures from tired Bible stories. Through all of that and moving through the silent land of that place save for the realities of workmen sweating profundities as they worked, something stuck shifted in me and I resisted the inevitability of departure at the week's end. Another spiritual great is buried in the grounds and this place has become a global centre for learning the prayer techniques of one St Ignatius, nobleman turned holy sage who created spiritual practices to transform the way we look at the world. Now people come and stay for longer retreats, centred around an individual life as each guest is given a "guide" to help navigate their hearts and minds through the stubbornness of their past and present confrontations with themselves.

Here I walk out onto sunny heathlands, alone with myself. I eat and sleep, read and sit in each of the chapels, sensitively decorated with poignant pieces of writing, ambiguous sculptures which enable a variety of spiritual interpretations to rise. I listen to myself unfolding in the space, unnerving yet necessary. In a microcosm, it is the reconstruction, the restoration of a life, one pulled and tugged and bitten into by others' demands and needs and inability, which has now become a crushing overwhelm. I feel lucky then to have got away, to put that down, if only for a while. My parents used to visit a convent where there was a strong community of nuns. Those were the days of a capable and chosen life of holiness. There was a swing in a barn and I fell into hay which stuck in my chubby childhood thighs, a reminder of those prickly sins which children are so conscious of, and as we grow, they come at us in other ways that we learn to keep inside like the stubborn thorn which lies buried for years in our flesh.

Now the people before me I know not; they are complete strangers. But that is part of the beauty of this time—to go to the edges of our lives where no one knows us. People take themselves away from these for many reasons, tiredness, a knowledge that they are on the cusp of a new era. Unsure of which way to go, the belief is that a fresh space will help with that. That somehow there will be an echo of a knowledge they already know down in the unopened places of a life. Often it is an acknowledged recovery of a hurt as we, betrayed by who or what we believed would be vibrant or faithful throw an unexpected punch. Or it is the feeling of being slowly gnawed away, so that nothing is left much of the essence of ourselves. Our sense of loss immense, we cannot fathom how we have arrived at such a place of drought.

For me, here, it is demanding work though for I am leading the retreat. I offer two talks each day for four days, offer time with those who have come as often there is safety and a different delight in sharing with a stranger. My own solace comes from walks in fields, passing trees with laden plums in golden sunlight, deep in this verdant valley where we eat the estate's lamb for dinner and drink homemade gin but all in a covenanted silence which restores. There is a labyrinth to walk into and out from, woodland benches to sit on, hidden glades to stand still. Here is a way for me to see beyond the now of my own demanded life.

With my small group I share images, invite them to explore passages from the Bible and stories. "I offer what I offer", I tell them; they do not have to come and listen to my content, but they do, and I hope so keenly that what I share does not lead them into further hurt or tiredness. In this place there is a rule of no clergy "shop talk". The atmosphere is noncompetitive; there is no blustering, name dropping, no "look what I've achieved in my shiny and successful church". Here is a place to bring our failure and our frailty, shared or not. We know one another only by our first names. I do not know who is a bishop or a farmer, married or divorced, sick or well. It is a relief to not be owned and public, if only for a while.

There is a great need in our age of stressed pressures to get away from how our lives have become. We no longer waste time to empty our minds, to think deeply about things, to ruminate, to grow wisdom because we are busy utilizing every waking moment. My church treasurer sends me emails at one in the morning. I am simultaneously worried for his wellbeing and secretly grateful for all the work he does to try to keep our parish on a healthy financial track. But I want to model a sustainable way for us all to be human and do that well. Retreat houses are good at this, they understand our human tendency to keep up, to hold things up.

There is a move to build places of sanctuary in ordinary life as well. To make that manageable for those who are too busy or too poor to be able to step away and take soul rest. Retreats in Daily Life are popular these days, ways of intentionally building prayer and a sense of God into a life if only we have the discipline to keep it there. Retreat houses are repair shops for the souls. Here is space to make sense of the world again, to walk back through the doors with heads held high.

2 6

The funeral

I am here again. Leading the funeral for a family who have lost three of their members over the last year. The deceased—45—has been someone everyone loved, and when I ask how he died no one is quite sure yet; the coroner's report is expected soon.

I have grown to love this family. They are a rag-tag bunch of colourful people, many with significant vulnerabilities and with the relationships within the clan unclear. They are dressed in everyday clothes, trainers and mismatched colours in clothes that don't fit too well. Some of them look dishevelled and some have surreptitious sucks of roll up fags or vapes. One with messy hair and a gap in his teeth, another in a cardigan in sage green, bobbly and drab. I remain unsure who is related to who, someone who looks like a son is in fact a brother. The concept of family here extends (and then afterwards contracts) like a well-played accordion, got out for the party and then put away again until the next rite of passage. Part of the complexity stems from the fact that the matriarch and second husband (one of the ones I have buried) also fostered over 70 kids—a remarkable fact of generous love. Getting to know this family is like feeling my way in the dark into a subterranean cave network, channels and passageways which all strangely meet up somewhere in the centre.

But this crew know one another, and camaraderie spreads around the scattered group, like warm air on a summer's day. Really, it is their show, not mine or even God's. I am smiled at by some as they recognize me, relieved at least that the cleric is familiar territory. But for the most part I am ignored. I stand slightly apart, in my black and white robes, like a tolerant penguin, patiently waiting for the colony to decide it is ready to walk to the shores of the sea or, in this case, church. It is the kind of crowd where people often feel unsure about entering the building itself, needing safety of numbers and unsure of what might be expected in a place and culture which feels as alien as a betting shop would be for me. I simply would not know what to do.

The hearse arrives. Since being back in parish ministry funerals seem to have changed. No large black limousine here, older men, usually part of the same respectable family who hold onto a reputation of "doing things well" in a neighbourhood. There is still something trusted about a man in his early sixties, polished brogues and top hat, who possesses the formality yet kindliness of an old-fashioned grandfather. But here the funeral car is a white Nissan Leaf—tiny in comparison to the monster corteges of the past and has been specially designed to hold a coffin, driver and one or two passengers. It's compact and trendy and the funeral directors are an all-girl team called "A Natural Undertaking". Their website says they offer funerals that are "Simple, modern, traditional, green or completely bespoke—the choice is yours". Begun by two friends, their aim was that funerals could be done differently, a decisive move away from traditional black sombre ceremonies with the perception that grieving should be buttoned up, locked inside the coffin itself. No black top and tails here, Suzy and Carrie arrive adorned in bright scarves, spotty dresses and today in leopard print shoes. They are kind, perfectly professional and clearly have things in hand, a perfect match for the bunch that have rocked up at church.

The deceased (Jimmy) lays cold and stiff in a white cardboard coffin. It has rope handles and has been decorated by the family with all manner of messages in felt tip, photos, flowers and memorabilia. It reminds me of a homemade birthday cake, personal and with a wondrous "owned" quality to it, somehow speaking of life and celebration rather than someone who is being buried far too young.

This kind of gig is well within my comfort zone. I have been leading funerals for over 20 years, and this group are just grateful to be here and for me to lead something we call "the service". Officially as Church of England vicar I have to include certain elements which indeed we have—a Bible passage, the Lord's Prayer, set texts we call "liturgy", words which are meant to "send someone on their way". But here, this service is an eclectic fusion of spiritualities. The service contains certain elements which might be considered "dodgy" theologically to some Christian leaders who are more conservative than I. So, amongst this family, is a belief in the power of crystals and the presence of angels, and at the end we listen to Nyabinghi drumming, a form of percussion which is meant to summon the spirits of the dead to life again. But in an age of fused spiritualities, as well as in the context of where we live, this feels a natural part of the opportunity we offer to help people when someone dies. It is forgotten too, that so much of established religion is an overlay of so-called paganism or "natural religion". Pushing those elements out of an allowed and existing worship means also pushing out all that was rich and wise about these ancient belief systems.

And it does not bother me because what matters to these folk is still to hold their service in a traditional church building. As Anglicans we have a responsibility to enable anyone in our parish to do this, or, as in this case, if our buildings hold special meaning. Pastorally, church becomes an artery to provide a ritual and space to say goodbye and to help soothe grief. And if we care and are in touch with the neighbourhood where we are living and loving people, then we learn what the expectations might be. Here, in my context and city of super-diversity, a place where the professionals mix with the creatives, I sense that there will not be many offended by what is offered. All that matters today is that I show and generate an atmosphere where warmth and genuineness can be shown and shared. There is a line in the stories of Jesus where he looks at the crowd and feels they are like lost sheep without a shepherd. These folk are not so lost perhaps but I feel a sense of loyalty and huge compassion as their temporary shepherd.

This morning, I have also been brave, allowing the family to have ten minutes where anyone can get up and share their special memories about the deceased. But I have planned with the sister who organized the service—if anyone gets carried away, I will get up and continue. There is still that recognized understanding of the authority of she who is clergy. We begin the "open space". The daughter speaks first. She is poised, dressed in white suit with gold earring squares so huge they bump against her shoulders. She is about 20, the same age as my daughter, but she looks after her younger brother, the child of another member of this family. She has been so grateful for everything, and I have hugged her a lot. Next, a grandmother speaks, then a best mate who gets us all to yell the name of the deceased at top volume. It is odd yet natural, I cannot gauge my own response of initial irritation as no one asked my permission about whether it is appropriate to behave like this in church, but the speech is so sincere I cannot object. Then a woman with a patterned coat of art gets up. She tells a story of how Jimmy had travelled across the city years ago, to sit quietly at the foot of her bed as she was recovering from an operation in hospital. Unaware for most of this visit, as he got up to travel back home and as darkness fell, she realized who he was. "There aren't many people", the speaker concluded, "who would spend an hour of their time just sitting at the foot of the bed of a friend without you even knowing they had been there." Another got up, Mrs Green apparently, a stocky woman with a strong Caribbean accent. She is dressed smartly, complete with cream hat and shoes. Mrs Green, in a voice which would rival many a street preacher, is off. She speaks up and out, of the fact that the deceased was such a loving person, of how he would do anything for anyone and that our job now is to perpetuate the person that he was in how we behave. Even if it is an exaggeration (as many a eulogy often is), she's on fire and does better than me, rousing the congregation who whoop in with "Amens" and applause.

But the ten minutes is up, and we need to get to the crematorium, the final part of Mr James Summers' journey in this world, even though I believe he has already moved onto the next. I get up, deliver my thoughts (perfectly acceptable theology) and in a moment of spontaneity, tell them that actually they don't need me, for through their beautiful contributions they have described a way of life which feels already priestly—that of sitting by a bedside, kindness showed in a life and the continuation of love after death. Good on them. It dilutes the arrogant assumption of the professional religious that clergy are indispensable.

We gather outside. I lead the coffin out to the Nissan Leaf hearse with a pulsating beat box playing a pop song from the 1980s. We stand around on this urban street with its litter, as the bearers manoeuvre the coffin back into the car. They stand, people used to waiting for the NHS or benefit queue, not a black suit amongst them except from a member of our congregation who sidles up to me and says, "Good job. I forget that this is what you guys do in the week." What else did he think we do, I wondered on reflection? It was that classic ignorance that somehow we clerics just work on Sundays, and he, attending church for years, really should know better.

2 7

Reverence

I have just watched a meditative and heartfelt documentary called *The Nettle Dress*. The ordinary sounding Allan Brown is a textile artist and, after the death of his beloved wife, begins a seven-year endeavour to weave a hand-spun dress from stinging nettles foraged in the woods surrounding his home. The dress took 4,267 metres of thread, and Brown appears throughout the film like some kind of ancient Briton, creating a genuinely sustainable piece of clothing, Viking-style, which his daughter models in a fairy-tale like scene at the end of the film. There is something powerful about the weaving of something strong and sustainable out of a plant renowned for inflicting pain. I still remember how my body felt when I fell off a swing somewhere in my childhood, into a very large patch of nettles. And there is something interesting about taking a nondescript, insignificant plant, understanding its hidden qualities, and creating something alleviative from it. Foraging is fashionable these days—free food and full of vitamins; nettles, for example, contain much iron and you can make soup out of their young leaves. There is something understood by many of us too, about how a person works grief through, and in this case, the natural world aids that process. Healing happens, never completely, but the wearing of the dress by Allan Brown's daughter becomes an inheritance where life can continue.

As a priest I absorb people's pain too and try to do something with it, try without easy placations but inherited wisdom to provide a way forward for another. You must be very patient, something I am not always good at. Not one of us, in the end, can escape troubles in our lives, the loss of loved ones being probably the worst. But what I recognized in this film is the continuous challenge to glimpse possibility—of potential, of healing within the ordinary and often, like the humble nettle, the nondescript. Through the process of that, however it happens, and however long it takes, redemption and so many other words we associate with the spiritual, play out.

The children in our local church school call me "Reverend Magdalen". The dictionary definition of "reverence" is a feeling of profound respect for someone or something. This generic title for clergy goes back centuries and the higher you climb up the ladder of clerical promotion (at least as an Anglican) the more titles you are endowed with. For centuries it was this title of "Reverend" that was associated with the *person*. And today in the discernment process, which is often long and rigorous, would-be clergy are challenged to think about what it means to inhabit personal holiness, to carry the right to indeed be described as "Reverend". And that of course is right—we who represent God and Church with capital "C" need to sustain the reputation of both, in being and body. But it is also a huge and sometimes oppressive responsibility for priests are human too. They get angry, drink too much, lust after those they are not married to, swear, are unkind, greedy and selfish. They also cannot always be "nice".

In my 28 years of ordained ministry, I hope I have earned my own title even though I continue to feel unworthy of it. On many days, I often do not feel very "Reverend". Instead, I feel mischievous, edgy, weary and damaged, bearing inner scars from silted hurts that might never heal. But I have also learnt that all of that is good, for what it means is that I am living a life just like everyone else, loving too much at times, making mistakes, trying to decipher God in a life and through that doing some good. All that makes me approachable as well as relatable and it opens opportunities for people to explore some of the things that matter.

I try to hold my own reverence each day, to pray and care and behave transparently as well as thoughtfully, so that others will indeed understand something of the title I carry. But much more important to me is that through all that I am, as well as what I do, I can enable and encourage others to see the reverence which is woven into the world. To learn, or relearn, that is also a calling towards becoming more loving. For I have found that every moment of inner or outer rage or cynicism ages me, but that every act of love has the capacity to expand not only myself but also inspires others to do so too. Every expression of reverence brings me closer to eternity, of experiencing the mystery of why we are here and how we must be with one another and of seeing the beauty always in the world. There is really nothing more to it than this. For all the theology I have read, the prayers I have said, the creeds I've stated, what divine life and living a faith-filled life means, is increasingly distilled. As Teresa of Avila put it, "The more mature one becomes on the spiritual pathway, the simpler God becomes."

My friend Nicola, Methodist minister and generally wonderful human being, is one such fellow "Reverend". We have known each other a long time. We know one another well, warts and all, we listen to each other in genuine non-judgment and recognize how hard, as well as fulfilling, ministry can feel these days. She is always interesting, and I never tire of being in her presence. We get on so well because we share similar attitudes to life. She is creative and approaches most things with vitality and vigour, has done some unusual things, living in Russia for six years being one of these, and she has never lost her love of travelling. Last year Nicola spent two weeks with the Academy of Spiritual Formation, spending time with communities of migrants trying to cross the border from Mexico into Arizona state, USA. She wrote this fabulous poem, and it is published with kind permission from the author for the first time. It is set with a backdrop of images of migrant people she took during her time there.

> They are everywhere, as far as the eye can see.
> Some might describe them as hordes or swarms.
> I don't know what the collective name for them is
> —or even if there is one.
> Each one is different, unique.
> Some of them are straight.
> Others aren't.
> Some are solitary.
> Others are in groups.
> Some of them have open arms. They reach out . . .
> —perhaps in prayer or praise . . .
> ——perhaps in welcome or invitation.
> ———or as a way of establishing boundaries and claiming their space.

I would like to embrace them—but that will be painful.
I guess love across a prickly protective barrier always hurts.

They are not migrants.
They don't move.
Although I heard of one who toppled and killed the man who shot at it.

I don't know much about them.
But I love them—each one of them.
I guess that, if I lived here all the time,
I might just take them for granted and stop noticing them.

But this week I get to spend time with them.
to be a guest in their home ...
to learn from them,
my brother cacti,
how to be silent and still,

how to stand tall,
rooted to the earth and reaching to the skies,
how to share the land with all that God has formed and made.

Nicola Vidamour

By the time we have finished reading, we realize that the poem actually describes cacti rather than those who are migrating from one country to another, as the images on Nicola's YouTube video of the poem also depict. However, the poem is brilliantly constructed in such a way that it could be about both migrants as well as cacti. The author sees the inextricable dignity in both, displaced human beings and in these ancient, prickly plants. Both for her are endowed with a deep reverence. She does what all good priests are called to do then, to seek and then to illuminate that this reverence is deeply within everything in this universe. Everything is fused with the glory of the divine in some shape or form. She calls these spiky plants "brothers" and says that she loves each one of them. Indeed, through this love they teach her so much—of how to be still and silent, of how to be a guest in that place, of how to share God-space, which is not any of ours to own or control.

For this is also the life of the priest or "minister", as her church describes her. That through this revelation of reverence we are drawn to offer love to whoever and whatever steps across the path. This "calling", or inspiration is in fact open to every human person, regardless of ethnicity, age or faith; and here lies everyone's earthly vocation.

Milton Keynes UK
Ingram Content Group UK Ltd.
UKHW020634111124
450921UK00011B/99

9 781789 593617